Planning and Managing Drupal Projects

Dani Nordin

D1472187

O'REILLY®

Beijing · Cambridge · Farnham · Köln · Sebastopol · Tokyo

Planning and Managing Drupal Projects

by Dani Nordin

Copyright © 2011 Dani Nordin. All rights reserved.
Printed in the United States of America.

Published by O'Reilly Media, Inc., 1005 Gravenstein Highway North, Sebastopol, CA 95472.

O'Reilly books may be purchased for educational, business, or sales promotional use. Online editions are also available for most titles (*http://my.safaribooksonline.com*). For more information, contact our corporate/institutional sales department: (800) 998-9938 or *corporate@oreilly.com*.

Editor: Julie Steele	**Cover Designer:** Karen Montgomery
Production Editor: Jasmine Perez	**Interior Designer:** David Futato
Proofreader: O'Reilly Production Services	**Illustrator:** Robert Romano

ISBN: 978-1-449-30548-2

[LSI]

1315876858

Table of Contents

Preface

If you're reading this book, you're probably a web designer who has heard of Drupal, wants to get started with it, and may have even tried it out a couple of times. And you might be frustrated because even if you're used to code, Drupal has thrown you a major learning curve that you hadn't expected. And just when you think you've gotten a basic site together, now you have to figure out how to make it *look* right—and the whole process starts over again.

Yep, I've been there too. That's why I wrote this book.

This book is for the solo site builder or small team that's itching to do interesting things with Drupal, but needs a bit of help understanding how to set up a successful Drupal project. It's for the designer who knows HTML and CSS, but doesn't want to have to learn how to speak developer in order to parse Drupal documentation. Most importantly, this book is for those who want to use Drupal to make their vision a reality, but need help working their minds around the way that Drupal handles design challenges.

Contents of This Book

What I present here are not recipes for specific use cases; although recipes can be useful, experience has shown there's rarely just one way to accomplish an objective in Drupal. Rather, what I'm offering is context: a way of understanding what Drupal is and how it works, so that you can get over the hump and start figuring things out on your own.

This book, Planning and Managing Drupal Projects, is part of a three-part series (look for *Design and Prototyping for Drupal* and *Development Tricks for Drupal Designers*, coming soon). Over the course of this series, collectively titled *Drupal for Designers*, I'll help you understand:

- How to plan and manage Drupal projects successfully (in the *Planning and Managing* guide);
- How to more effectively create visual design for Drupal by understanding what Drupal is spitting out (in *Design and Prototyping*);

- How to break down your design layouts to turn them into Drupal themes (in *Design and Prototyping*);
- How to get started with version control, Drush, and other ninja-developer Drupal Magick that can make your life much easier working with Drupal (in *Development Tricks for Drupal Designers*).

In this first volume, *Planning and Managing Drupal Projects*, we'll look at the typical lifecycle of a Drupal project, with a focus on the early stages of planning a site. You will learn:

- How to understand what Drupal is doing "under the hood," including some basic terms you should know;
- The lifecycle of a typical Drupal project;
- How to get the information you need to effectively plan, estimate and manage a Drupal project;
- Techniques for framing the design challenge and dealing with the User Experience layer;
- Why you should always get real content for the project as early as possible;
- How to choose the right modules for your project (along with some of my favorite modules);
- How to walk clients through the Drupal design and development process.

A Caveat

The goal of this guide isn't to teach specific project management techniques. Every Drupal team and site builder has their own approach to creating projects, and it's hard to pin down one "right" way to create in Drupal. The key to appropriate planning, then, is:

1. **Knowing what you have to create**. This is where the site planning and discovery process, discussed in Chapter 2, is especially useful.

2. **Knowing what you'll need to do in order to get the job done**. This will vary depending on the project, but there are some important factors to consider in Chapter 3.

3. **Knowing how to walk clients through the process**. In Chapter 4, I share some of my experience from years of working with clients, including proposing and estimating projects, handling difficult conversations, and creating effective documentation.

In the last chapter, I share some of the client documentation I've developed over six years of running a design studio and estimating Drupal projects. The content is available under Creative Commons, so you are free to use and adapt it as you like.

Conventions Used in This Book

The following typographical conventions are used in this book:

Italic
> Indicates file names, directories, new terms, URLs, clickable items in the interface such as menu items and buttons, and emphasized text.

Constant width
> Indicates parts of code, contents of files, commands, and output from commands.

Constant width italic
> Indicates user input.

 This icon signifies a tip, suggestion, or general note.

 This icon indicates a warning or caution.

Using Code Examples

This book is here to help you get your job done. In general, you may use the code in this book in your programs and documentation. You do not need to contact us for permission unless you're reproducing a significant portion of the code. For example, writing a program that uses several chunks of code from this book does not require permission. Selling or distributing a CD-ROM of examples from O'Reilly books does require permission. Answering a question by citing this book and quoting example code does not require permission. Incorporating a significant amount of example code from this book into your product's documentation does require permission.

We appreciate, but do not require, attribution. An attribution usually includes the title, author, publisher, and ISBN. For example: "*Planning and Managing Drupal Projects* by Dani Nordin. Copyright 2011 O'Reilly Media, Inc., 978-1-449-30548-2."

If you feel your use of code examples falls outside fair use or the permission given above, feel free to contact us at *permissions@oreilly.com*.

Safari® Books Online

Safari Books Online is an on-demand digital library that lets you easily search over 7,500 technology and creative reference books and videos to find the answers you need quickly.

With a subscription, you can read any page and watch any video from our library online. Read books on your cell phone and mobile devices. Access new titles before they are available for print, and get exclusive access to manuscripts in development and post feedback for the authors. Copy and paste code samples, organize your favorites, download chapters, bookmark key sections, create notes, print out pages, and benefit from tons of other time-saving features.

O'Reilly Media has uploaded this book to the Safari Books Online service. To have full digital access to this book and others on similar topics from O'Reilly and other publishers, sign up for free at *http://my.safaribooksonline.com*.

How to Contact Us

Please address comments and questions concerning this book to the publisher:

O'Reilly Media, Inc.
1005 Gravenstein Highway North
Sebastopol, CA 95472
800-998-9938 (in the United States or Canada)
707-829-0515 (international or local)
707-829-0104 (fax)

We have a web page for this book, where we list errata, examples, and any additional information. You can access this page at:

http://www.oreilly.com/catalog/9781449305482

To comment or ask technical questions about this book, send email to:

bookquestions@oreilly.com

For more information about our books, courses, conferences, and news, see our website at *http://www.oreilly.com*.

Find us on Facebook: *http://facebook.com/oreilly*

Follow us on Twitter: *http://twitter.com/oreillymedia*

Watch us on YouTube: *http://www.youtube.com/oreillymedia*

Acknowledgments

To be honest, I'm still amazed at being given the chance to write these books. It had been swirling around in my mind for a while, and I consider it one of life's happier coincidences that I happened to get the opportunity to write about Drupal in not one, but two major book projects this year.

A brief list of thanks to the folks who have helped me in various capacities to help this book see the light of day:

My intrepid editors, Julie Steele and Meghan Blanchette, for giving me the opportunity to write the book, and for helping me make sense of O'Reilly's lengthy style guide. Also thanks to Laurel Ruma for making the introduction to Julie so I could actually *sell* this crazy idea.

Todd Nienkerk of Four Kitchens (fourkitchens.com (*http://fourkitchens.com*)) helped me understand how the ideas I've used in really tiny teams apply to the work of larger teams; his feedback as a reviewer (as indicated by the many times I quote him throughout this text), was invaluable.

Tricia Okin of Papercut (papercutny.com (*http://papercutny.com*)) was instrumental in helping me deconstruct what my readers would need. She also provided a tremendous real-world example for the book in the form of the *Urban Homesteaders Unite* project. Her commentary throughout this process, as well as her wicked sense of humor and willingness to actually learn Drupal, has been a constant source of awesome.

Various colleagues and professional acquaintances, in and out of the Drupal community, who were kind enough to let me interview them: Greg Segall of OnePica, Richard Banfield of Fresh Tilled Soil, David Rondeau of inContext Design, Todd Nienkerk, Jason Pamental, Amy Seals, Mike Rohde, Ryan Parsley, Leisa Reichelt and Andrew Burcin.

Claudio Luis Vera, for introducing me to Drupal, and being a mentor, collaborator, and commiserator for the last several years. Also, Ben Buckman of New Leaf Digital, who has been one of the guiding forces behind my passion to bring Drupally knowledge —particularly Drush, Git and other stuff—to my fellow designers.

Finally, I want to thank the niecelet, Patience Marie Nordin, for giving me someone to be a role model to, and my husband, Nicolas Malyska, for being the most supportive partner anyone can hope for.

About the Author

Dani Nordin is an independent user experience designer and strategist who specializes in smart, human-friendly design for progressive brands. She discovered design purely by accident as a Theatre student at Rhode Island College in 1995, and has been doing some combination of design, public speaking and writing ever since.

Dani is a regular feature at Boston's Drupal meetup, and is a regular speaker at Boston's Design for Drupal Camp. In 2011, she was one of several contributors to *The Definitive Guide to Drupal 7* (Apress); the *Drupal for Designers* series is her second book project. You can check out some of her work at tzk-design.com (*http://tzk-design.com*). She also blogs almost regularly at daninordin.com (*http://daninordin.com*).

Dani lives in Watertown, MA with her husband Nick, and Persephone, a 14-pound ~~giant ball of black furry love~~ cat. Both are infinite sources of comedic gold.

About the Reviewers

Todd Ross Nienkerk, Four Kitchens co-founder, has been involved in the web design and publishing industries since 1996. As an active member of the Drupal community, Todd regularly speaks at Drupal events and participates in code sprints all over the world. (In the last three years, he has spoken at 20 conferences and attended five code sprints in seven countries.) Todd is a member of the Drupal Documentation Team and recently co-chaired the Professional Drupal Services track for DrupalCon Copenhagen 2010 and chaired the Design/UX track for DrupalCon Chicago 2011. As a member of the Drupal.org (*http://drupal.org*) Redesign Team, Todd helped spearhead the effort to redesign Drupal.org (*http://drupal.org*) and communicate a fresher, more effective Drupal brand.

Tricia Okin is a designer based and working in Brooklyn since 2001 and founded **papercut** in 2004. **papercut** was resurrected in early 2009 by Tricia after realizing she wanted to make good work with tangibility and purpose. She also realized she couldn't and would rather not do it alone in a design vacuum. From there, Tricia called on the best resources she could find and mustered up a gang of wily collaborators with as much passion for being their own bosses as she has.

CHAPTER 1

Introduction

A Quick and Dirty Guide to DrupalSpeak™

If you're just starting off with Drupal, one of the hardest things to figure out is what people are saying when they discuss Drupal terms. What is a *Node*? What do you mean, *Taxonomy*? The list below is a quick and dirty guide to DrupalSpeak™, which is a tongue-in-cheek way of describing Drupal's unique jargon. It includes the most common terms you'll find people using when they talk about Drupal.

Drupal Core (or Core Drupal)
>   The actual Drupal files that you downloaded from Drupal.org (*http://drupal.org*). *Drupal Core* is also used to talk about any functionality that is native to Drupal.

Contrib
>   Modules or themes that you install after you install Drupal Core.

sites/all
>   A folder within your Drupal installation which contains all the files, including any contrib modules or themes, that are being used to customize your site.

 Any module, theme, or other customization that you create for your site should always reside in *sites/all*.

Node
>   A single piece of content. This could be a news item, event listing, simple page, blog entry — you name it. Anything in your site that has a heading and a bit of text is a node. Nodes can also have custom fields, which are useful for all sorts of things. Think of a Node the way you would a page on a website, or a record in an address book.

Field

Fields are one of the best things about creating content in Drupal. Using fields, you can attach images or files to content, create extra descriptors (like a date for an event, or a subheading for an article), or even reference other nodes. Drupal core (as of Drupal 7) allows for a number of field formats, but certain formats—such as images, file uploads, or video—require you to install contrib modules. There's a list of contrib modules to extend fields' power and usefulness in the Modules chapter.

Block

A piece of reusable content such as a sidebar menu, advertising banner, or callout box. Blocks can be created by a View (see Figure 1-1) or other contributed modules or created by hand in Drupal's Blocks administration menu. The beauty of blocks is the flexibility of display—you can set up blocks to display based on any criteria that you set. This is especially helpful on home pages, for example, or for displaying a menu that's only relevant to a specific section of a website.

Content type

The type of node you're creating. One of Drupal's best features is its support of multiple content types, each of which can be sorted out and displayed by any number of criteria. For example, in a basic corporate site, you might have the following content types: Blog Post, Basic Page, Event, News Item, Testimonial. Each of these content types can be sorted out and organized, using Views (see below), to create the Blog section, Events Page, News Room, etc. Best of all, your client can easily update the Events page simply by adding a new *Event*. Drupal will do all the work of sorting out the Events page and archiving old events.

Taxonomy

Content categories. At its most basic level, you can think of taxonomy as tags for content (like blog entries). The true power of taxonomy, however, lies in organizing large quantities of content by how an audience might search. For example, a recipe site can use taxonomy to organize recipes by several criteria—type of recipe (dessert, dinner, etc.), ingredients (as tags), and custom indicators (vegetarian, vegan, gluten-free, low carb, etc.). In building the site, you could then use Views to allow users to search by or filter recipes by any one (or several) of these criteria.

Users, Roles and Permissions

Users are exactly what they sound like: people or organizations that have registered on your site. The key to working with users lies in roles; Drupal allows you to create unique roles for anything that might need to happen on your site, and set permissions for each role depending on what that role might need to do. For example, if you're creating a magazine-type site with multiple authors, you might want to create a role called "author" that has permission to access, create and edit their own content, but nobody else's. You might also create a role called "editor" that has access to edit, modify and publish or unpublish the content of any of the authors.

Module

A plugin that adds functionality to your site. Out of the box, Drupal provides a strong framework, but the point of the framework is to add functionality to it using modules. Drupal.org/project/modules (*http://drupal.org/project/modules*) has a list of all the modules that have been contributed by the Drupal community, sorted by most popular.

View

An organized list of individual pieces of content that you create within the site, using the Views module. This allows you to display content related to taxonomy or content type, such as a "view" of blog posts versus a "view" of events.

Theme

The templates that control the look and feel of a Drupal site. Drupal core comes with several themes that are very useful for site administration and prototyping; however, custom themes should always reside in your sites/all/themes folder and not in the core themes folder, located at *themes* in your Drupal files.

Template files (`*.tpl.php`*)*

Individual PHP files that Drupal uses for template generation. Most Drupal themes will have, at the very least, a tpl.php for blocks, nodes, and pages. Once you get the hang of working with tpl.phps, you can create custom templates for anything from a specific piece of content or specific content types to the output of a specific view.

Talking to Clients About Drupal

When talking about Drupal to clients, the biggest mistake you can make is to start talking to them about Blocks and Nodes and Views, and using other DrupalSpeak™. While some clients actually do understand this stuff, it's been my experience the majority of them don't, and frankly, it's not their job to know it. I've had this argument with many a well-meaning Drupaller, who insists that "educating" the client is actually useful, but I see the same result every time someone tries: start speaking to a client about Taxonomy and Views, and watch his/her eyes glaze over.

My favorite way to talk to clients about Drupal is to start with the concept of a News page or blog homepage. Each individual post is its own piece of content, with its own fields, categories and tags, and Drupal's job is to organize that content on the page for you. The client's job (or their copywriter's) is to give you those individual pieces of content, with all their various fields, categories and tags, so that you can put them into the system and set up the rules for how they're organized.

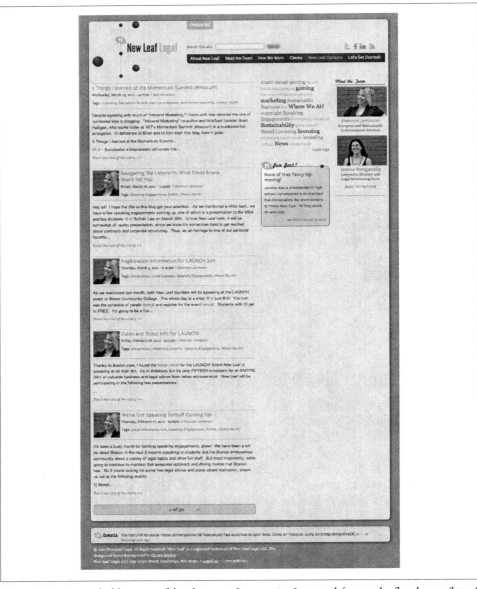

Figure 1-1. A sample blog page (like this one, from a site I created for newleaflegal.com (http://newleaflegal.com)) is a great way to start explaining the concept of Nodes, Taxonomy, Views and Blocks to your clients. Just don't call them that.

Organizing Your Files

As noted above, any customizations to your site (modules, themes, etc.) should reside in your *sites/all* or *sites/default* folder. There are many reasons for this, but the most important one is for ease of upgrading your site. When upgrading Drupal core, you're essentially replacing all of the files in your Drupal installation with the newest version of the files, and updating the database to reflect the new configuration. By keeping all of your customizations in the *sites* folder, you lessen the risk that all of your files will be replaced once you update. Another handy facet of using the *sites* folder to hold all your customizations is ease of editing; by keeping everything in one place, there's less to hunt through when you're looking to change a file.

By default, you should keep all your customizations in *sites/all*. If you're dealing with a single site, it's just as easy to keep things in *sites/default*, but if you ever get into creating multi-site installations (which is way beyond the scope of this book), being in the habit of keeping everything in *sites/all* will save your bacon. You also need to organize your code according to what it does; for example, themes should go into *sites/all/themes*, modules in *sites/all/modules*, etc. This is because Drupal actually looks for themes in a folder called *themes*, modules in a folder called *modules*, etc. If you don't have things stored in the appropriate folder, everything goes to heck.

Lifecycle of a Drupal Project

A good project plan for Drupal starts with the client. How much do they know about Drupal? Did they specifically request it, or was it something you suggested to them as you heard their list of requirements? This is surprisingly important information. For clients who are new to Drupal or just learning about it, there's a bit more handholding you need to do in order to get them on board with the process. Designing for content management systems is very different from designing for Flash or with straight HTML; it's very common for Drupal designers to realize too late that the brilliant layout they designed won't go into Drupal without a serious fight.

I typically break Drupal projects up into six distinct phases:

1. **Discovery**. During discovery, we learn as much as we can about the client, the project, and the project's objectives. This is also where we start to create a map of the functionality that we need to implement, any resources we'll need, etc.

2. **User Experience & Architecture**. This is where we take a deep dive into the lives, personalities, and other factors that define the humans that will need to deal with this project on a daily basis—both the end users that visit the site, and the clients who will end up managing the content once the project is finished. During this phase, you'll be doing work like wireframes, user flows, and often starting to prototype things directly into Drupal.

3. **Prototyping**. During prototyping, usually done just prior to starting the Functional Implementation phase, we start testing some of the hypotheses and user flows that came out of the User Experience phase. For simple sites, the prototyping and functional implementation phase go together; for more complex user flows, or for projects where you're wrangling a ton of content, the prototyping phase is essential to making sure that something you want to create will work the way you want it to in Drupal. We'll go deeper into prototyping in a future guide, *Design and Prototyping for Drupal*.

4. **Functional Implementation**. During this phase, the focus is on creating the functionality that we've described in the user experience phase, and ironing out any areas where the functionality we've decided on doesn't make sense, or aren't available within the budget. For many smaller sites, there's a good chance that you'll be doing this work on your own; however, if you're not currently on a Drupal team, be advised: get to know some developers, and pay them to do things for you when you're in a rut. Developers are a Drupal designer's best friend.

5. **Visual Design and Theming**. Notice, please, that visual design, here defined as the colors, fonts, images and other branding elements that define the look and feel of a given site, comes fifth in this list. There are many reasons for this, most of which you'll find in this book. The most important, however, is because bringing visual design into the picture too early in a Drupal project—or any significant project, for that matter—is a recipe for disaster. Part of your job as a Drupal designer is to keep clients focused on what's important, and what's important is how this site will serve their business objectives and their brand. While visual design is an important component of the site's value, it's just one piece of it—and it's the piece that clients will most often fixate on, to the detriment of more important issues, such as whether a user actually needs 50 pages of content in order to make a purchasing decision. The best way to explain this to clients is that the first part of the process—*which is still design, by the way*—sets up the experience you're creating for the user, and establishes content priorities. The visual design/theming phase makes sure that the experience you design in those early phases meshes with the client's brand and messaging.

6. **Testing and Launch**. Note to self: Always Test Before Launch. And After Launch. And then again after the client's had a chance to muck around with it. There are a few steps to the launch phase. First, you're moving your code from a development server to a staging server (the server that holds your site before the world gets to see it), and making sure parts didn't break in transit. Once you're sure everything's good, you'll move everything from staging to production (where the site will ultimately live). For this process, it's incredibly useful to have developers on your team.

For most projects, I also like to include a final phase, which helps consolidate everything that we've learned from working on the project:

7. **Wrap-up meeting/Documentation**. In the wrap-up meeting, you sit down with the client and discuss what worked well in the project, and what could have gone better. It's also a useful time to document the knowledge that you gained through the project, either in an internal Wiki for your team, or on Drupal.org (*http://drupal .org*) (**hint!**).

Figure 1-2 provides a quick visual breakdown of how a typical Drupal project works.

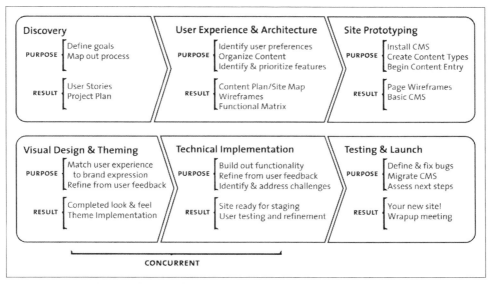

Figure 1-2. Typical project lifecycle for a Drupal site.

Implementation Plans: Breaking up your work

Another important issue to consider when talking to project stakeholders, and creating project plans, is how you categorize and prioritize your workflow. Since much of what you're doing in Drupal is managing content and/or creating specific functionality, it's vital to think, and speak, in terms of specific chunks of content or functionality that you have to create.

For example, Figure 1-3 shows the start of a functional matrix for Urban Homesteaders Unite (UHU), a Drupal project currently in process.

	A	B	C	D
1		Date	Task	Task Notes
2		**Task: Create and Post Events**		
3	▦		Create "Event" Content Type	Events will likely be imported from Eventbrite; need to add Category and Neighborhood taxonomy before publishing.
4	▦		"Event Types" taxonomy	Butchery, Urban Farming, Crafts, "Bikes, Bees & More", Cooking/Baking/Drinks, Canning & Preserving, DIY, Eco Home/Lifestyle
5	▦		"Neighborhood" taxonomy	
6	▦		"Location" taxonomy	Somerville/Cambridge, Brooklyn
7	▦		Test Eventbrite RSS integration	
8	▦		Document steps for Eventbrite registration	
9	▦		Configure Eventbrite RSS feeds	Need to look at Feeds module documentation; how to figure out mapping?
10	▦		Set up "event host" role	Permissions: post and edit events; access, create new Events feeds from Eventbrite.
11	▦		Create documentation page for posting events.	Step 1: Sign up for Drupal account. Step 2: Sign up for Eventbrite. Step 3. Create your first event. Step 4. Go to "My Events" and copy the RSS URL from that page. Step 5. Create new Events Feed with the Eventbrite URL.
12		**Task: Post Videos or Blogs**		
13	▦		Research on Video content type modules	What's the best option for 7? Do we want to stick with Youtube and Vimeo, or allow video uploads?
14	▦		Set up "contributor" role	Permissions to post and edit their own events and blogs
15	▦		Populate with sample content	
16	▦		Views: Create Video feed.	
17		**Task: Search Events**		
18	▦		Module: install Apache Solr	
19	▦		Views: Create view of events by location	

Figure 1-3. Functional matrix for Urban Homesteaders Unite (UHU). Note the specificity of tasks: Create a single taxonomy vocabulary or content type, rather than "all" content types.

By setting up your work this way, you eliminate the confusion that comes with making a statement like "on the week of the 14th, we're going to be setting up content types." While this can be perfectly fine if you only have a couple of content types to put together, any site that's larger than a few pages is likely to have enough complexity that each section of content or functionality will require its own content types, views, wireframes, and even custom page templates or modules—all of which will evolve during the course of the project.

By setting up the project plan with a list of very specific activities that will be done according to the tasks that must be accomplished on the site, you set a very reasonable expectation with your client on what they'll be able to see at the end of a given period of time. By breaking down the tasks in order of importance, you also help the development team get an idea of what the key user priorities are.

Most importantly, setting up project plans this way gives you the freedom to do whatever needs to be done to finish that specific task without having to waste time loading a bunch of milestones into Basecamp that the client doesn't really need to see.

Now that we have an idea of how a Drupal project will play out, it's time to go a bit deeper into what each phase looks like. In the next section, we focus on the Discovery phase, which sets the stage for user experience, and helps get everyone on the team (both you and the client) on the same page.

CHAPTER 2

Setting the Stage: Discovery and User Experience

In this chapter, we talk about one of the most important pieces of the Drupal puzzle, and the one that is often neglected by new site builders. The discovery process helps us gain an understanding of the client, the objectives of the project, and some of the functional issues that we might have to contend with; the user experience process helps us frame the interactions that will need to take place through the website, and helps everyone on the team agree about what we'll actually be creating.

Breaking Down the Project Goals

Every project, from the most basic promotional site to the most complex online community, should start with a solid *discovery* process. During discovery, you're looking to accomplish two things:

1. Find out everything you possibly can about the clients, their business goals, and why they want to invest in this project.
2. Create a set of documentation for the project that you can point to down the line to defend your design choices, and to help manage the inevitable "just one more thing..." conversations.

Every designer and team has a different process for discovery. Some like to have a quick meeting, sum it up with a few bullet points, and jump right into visual design concepts. Others need to take a deeper dive, and gather as much information as possible before doing anything other than very quick pencil sketches. I tend towards the deep dive approach. It not only helps me orient myself to the client's needs more effectively, but it gives me a well of information to draw from if I need to bring the client back to the same page down the road.

Project Discovery

The pre-estimate discovery phase (discussed in Chapter 4) gives you a chance to uncover the client's goals, establish some early functional priorities, and figure out how much work will be involved in creating their site, so you can provide a fair estimate of costs. During the project discovery phase, you'll add to that knowledge and wade deeper into the client's business goals, competitive landscape and other factors that will contribute to the design challenge.

The goal of this process is twofold:

1. To get a better understanding of the design challenge you're facing, and
2. To put together a series of documents that will guide the design process, and to which the client can agree to and sign off.

Getting client sign off on your assumptions is, arguably, the most important part of the discovery process. Whatever your personal opinion of user personas and other types of design documentation, the most important purpose they serve is giving you something to reference in the inevitable event that you have to defend a design decision you've made, or redirect a conversation away from "Is it really going to be that shade of blue?"

For example, several years ago I did an e-commerce site for an eco-friendly client. After moving through my standard discovery process and presenting the logo options I had put together, the client had agreed on a specific logo option, and we were ready to move into the next phase of the project. The next day, however, after discussing the logo with a couple of his colleagues, the client came back to tell me that something about the logo "didn't quite feel right."

Because we had established the client's business goals, audience profile and other requirements in the Project Planner (see Appendix A), the client and I were able to keep our conversation about the logo focused on the message that we were communicating (i.e. what this business is and who it serves), rather than on subjective preferences (i.e., whether he likes a particular font). By the end of the conversation, we had moved from having to redesign the logo completely to realizing that a couple of minor tweaks would integrate the design more effectively.

This is one of the most valuable aspects of design documents. Not only do they help you frame your design decisions, you can defend those decisions and more effectively deflect stakeholder requests that will derail the design or throw your production schedule into disarray.

A further note on documents

The type and amount of design documentation that you produce will likely depend on the project, the client and how they communicate. At a minimum, most projects will include any combination of the following:

- A Project Brief that establishes the site's communication goals, functional priorities and establishes standards for signoff and approvals.

 In Appendix A, you'll find the Project Brief I've adapted for my studio's projects.

- A set of user personas or scenarios that offer specific profiles of the site's intended users, mapped to specific goals and tasks that they need to accomplish.
- A preliminary site map that outlines the content that we expect to see on the site, and begins to establish a hierarchy for organizing it.
- A functional matrix that outlines specific tasks, functions, etc. the site needs to "do." Preferably, the matrix also prioritizes it against both its relevance to the user scenarios we've described, and the budget required to make it happen.
- Any number of user flows or concept drawings that help the design team understand how a user will interact with what we're creating.

All but the last set of documents I share and discuss directly with clients, and require them to approve before moving on. Concept drawings and user flows, although extremely helpful for solving user experience problems, have proven more important for me than for the client. In the next chapter, User Experience, we'll take a closer look at some of those documents.

Framing the Design Challenge

While the discovery phase sets up the client's objectives and perceptions of their audience, the *user experience* (UX) phase focuses on gaining a deeper understanding of the site's intended users, and works on framing the design challenge you're facing for the client and the development team.

The tangible deliverables of this phase may vary from team to team, but they often include things like:

- User personas or scenarios
- An outline, or matrix of functional requirements
- Sketches of screen designs or user flows
- Wireframes

- Paper or digital prototypes
- Content strategy documents, including a breakdown of site content, content types and categories. This may also include a breakdown of the site's user roles (editor, member, etc.) and what content they have permission to access, edit, etc.

The goal of this phase, which can take anywhere from a couple of days to a few months, is for the client and the development team to get on the same page regarding who the site's users are and why they are there. Additionally, and most importantly, the goal is to identify areas of the project where budget or project scope might need tweaking, and head off any confusion that might occur down the road.

Getting Your Hands Dirty with UX

Being a user experience designer in the Drupal community can be challenging. In many of the conversations I've had with designers and Drupal teams across the world, user experience deliverables are combined with project management activities, which can lead to a loss of focus on UX as the project moves forward and attention moves to time and resource management. Additionally, as the term *user experience* becomes more firmly established as an essential component of the web design puzzle, the question of what user experience actually means has become a topic of debate—and the Drupal community is certainly not an exception.

For the record, when I talk about *user experience*, I define it as:

- A set of design principles that focuses on learning about the actual people using a site in a *qualitative*, rather than a *quantitative*, way. Numbers can be useful for segmenting markets and planning a campaign; user experience requires observing real people, and seeing beyond statistics.
- A set of design principles that balances the needs of a business with the needs of their customers in a way that encourages a positive relationship.
- An activity that every member of the project team—from the official UX designer to project stakeholders—is responsible for, and that is best achieved by working collectively towards a common goal.

I do *not*, however, define *user experience* as:

- Creating a stack of wireframes or site maps in a vacuum.
- Creating and running usability tests.
- Creating a set of "personas" based on who you think your customers are without doing any kind of research, prototyping, or testing to back it up.
- A front-end developer who understands user experience methodologies, but doesn't understand the design principles underlying them.

While these different concepts can be *components* of user experience design, there's a distinct danger in considering any one of them to be the same idea.

Despite the challenges in defining the term, user experience designers are starting to make their mark on the Drupal community. More and more user-focused design firms are starting to embrace Drupal for projects, and the Drupal 7 redesign saw a huge number of usability improvements, led by UK-based designers Leisa Reichelt (*http://www.disambiguity.com/*) and Mark Boulton (*http://www.markboulton.co.uk/*). While there are still many improvements to be made, the fact that design and user experience are key components in the Drupal 8 project (see *http://drupal.org/community-initiatives/drupal-core/usability*), suggests that this issue is finally starting to gain traction among the Drupal community.

From the Trenches: Amy Seals, UI Architect

Amy Seals (http://www.projectsend.com/) works with Standing Cloud, a tech startup in Boulder, CO.

Dani: UX activities in Drupal projects often get lumped in with project management activities, so many UX designers find themselves thrust into project manager roles as well. How do you find your time split up when you're working on a team?

Amy: In theory, it should be sort of half-and-half, but I spend a lot more time on the Drupal side, doing the overall strategy. But then, day-to-day on a technical level, I end up in project management.

Dani: Which do you prefer?

Amy: I prefer the overall strategy. Watching something develop, and reacting to users, and anticipating their needs is what I prefer to focus on.

Dani: I think one of the biggest dangers in combining the UX and project managers' role is really on the clients' side. They don't necessarily get what a UX designer does...

Amy: Yes, I've seen that.

Dani: ...so, the fact that the project manager is discussing things like personas and user testing—things that are part of designing the user experience—they tend to lump all of that into project management and not think about how it relates to the user experience workflow.

Amy: Exactly. I think it's easier for people to see tactical things because they can see and measure immediate impact. Of course, you're going to have some short-term impacts as a result of UX work, but it's really kind of a long-term vision, and adaptation.

Dani: How successful have you been at selling the idea of UX design to your clients?

Amy: In my experience, the more complex the technology, the more willing a client is to trust your judgment about what needs to be done. Back in the early days, everybody knew what a website was, and there were these preconceived notions of how a website should work. With Drupal, there's so much complexity and capability that clients look for more guidance. But they also want to see results, so it's kind of a catch-22 in terms of how complex the system is and what you deliver within a reasonable time period.

Dani: Have you found any challenges with rapid iteration with Drupal, or clients having unreasonable expectations in terms of when things will be ready?

Amy: I've run into both ends of the gamut. Right now, our development cycle is about two weeks, because we are using Agile; but other places I've been, there's a tendency to forget that Drupal is very flexible, and very customizable, and you know: it is the web. It doesn't have to be perfect—and you shouldn't expect it to be perfect—because your users have yet to interact with it.

So we'd have these really long development cycles, and everybody would be really focused on these minute details that may or may not impact the overall user experience yet. There is this tendency towards trying to get things perfect, without really understanding what that is, or whether it can be done.

Dani: Some clients focus on incredibly minute details, and it is so much trouble getting them to understand that minor aesthetic details may make little difference to their user.

Amy: I find that breaking the project into smaller pieces, or smaller deliverables, has helped offset some of that focus on minutiae. Clients get overwhelmed with big-picture stuff, so they focus on very small details; if you can show them something like wireframes, for instance, or a user flow for a piece of technology, they can look at that, and think about it, and you can build on that instead of trying to constantly release these finished projects—or having the idea that you need a finished project in order to get client buy-in.

From a client perspective, I understand the desire for something that's more "finished" —you're committing a lot of time and money, and you want to make sure that what you get is what you need. If you don't see it until the end, it's a little scary.

Dani: What kind of user experience deliverables do you tend to build into a project? What kind of documentation do you build into a design cycle?

Amy: It depends on the project, and the client, of course, but some standard pieces are wireframes—those are a given for me. If you're starting something from the ground up, I tend to actually deliver UI [user interface] pieces, whether it's in Photoshop or something else.

If you have a project that's already underway, and you already have a look and feel set, I tend away from working in Photoshop, because it's more important for clients to get in and see how a user will use it, and be able to assess that, as opposed to spending time on visual elements.

For complicated functions—like if you have a process that's ongoing, whether it's an account creation or something else—I tend to do user flows as well, even before I wireframe, so that you and the client can make sure that you've covered all the pieces of that process. From a project management standpoint, it helps map out the project as well.

Dani: Have you ever worked with wireflows, where you create a user flow, but you're actually sharing samples of the screen, and the information required on each screen?

Amy: I've done a little bit of that. Based on the projects that I've worked with and the level of technical experience my clients have, if I break it down to blocks, like wireframes, it often works better than wireflows. I'll sometimes do a combination, too—I might do wireframes of a smaller component and say, "here's a screen which flows into this [other screen], and these are the components affected by this action, etc." But I'll keep it really minimal, so it strips out the noise.

Dani: Do you find that clients can't deal with the noise?

Amy: It seems to get in the way. Like you were saying, they're worried about a specific color of blue, and not really thinking about things like what a specific piece of content needs to say in order for the user to understand what's really going on—or even whether there's consistency within the interface.

So stripping out the noise, and getting down to the fundamentals of the interaction, I've found, helps. But when dealing with developers, it's a different scenario. They understand what's going on, and there tends to be less worry about that sort of noise.

Dani: Now, the flip side of that coin: do you find that it's very easy to strip out some noise, but insert the noise that Drupal gives you?

Amy: There is a certain level of noise that's inherent in the product. It's one of the things that's important to moving Drupal forward, and really building the long-term usability of the product from a community and from a client standpoint: educating your user about what to expect, and what things are important (and what things aren't). What noise is Drupal, and what noise is not? Slowly educating people on that is very important, because these are very powerful tools and you can lose track of them.

Dani: I also think it's important when talking to clients to know what they need to know versus what you need to know. There's this bare minimum of information that the client really needs, and half of the panic attacks that I see clients going through seem to come from somebody talking to them about all of these very Drupal-specific things.

Amy: I agree completely. I hadn't really thought about that. It's almost like you define your technical requirements for your developers, and then you have to translate that for your customers, and pick and choose what you show.

Dani: You have to translate Geek-Speak into Client-Speak. You become multi-lingual in a certain way, but it's especially true with UX. You have to be able to bring a bunch of people who don't necessarily speak the same language into the room together and say, "Okay, this is what we're doing."

Amy: I started out doing a lot of CRM, ERP and e-commerce, and integrating multiple platforms. So one of my roles has always been one of translator. And it's important, because you have to be able to articulate and communicate those things, and you have to be able to set a precedent for what the client needs to approve or check, and what *they're* going to be accountable for in the process.

There is a tendency with complex systems for some people to say "let us take care of the details; we're experts." We don't understand that the client needs to be accountable for the product from a very detailed point of view. They're not going to be worried about whether or not this page is delivered with Views or whatever, but they need to understand at a base level how things might work, because ultimately it's their product.

Dani: I also think that there's an expectation sometimes on the client side that you're the expert—you're going to have this figured out. And even with very complex systems, I've had clients who had stacks of documentation that they were surprised I hadn't read yet.

Amy: Exactly. They understand their customers, and so it's that middle ground, where you're a translator—but also, you have to be very much like a filter. The client is going to tell you a lot of things, so you have to decide, as a UX person, what is critical to convey through the interface to the user? It's a very overarching role, both translation and filtering. You're bridging the gap between a business, its customers, and the development team, and that sometimes can be a very big bridge.

Dani: So what have been the biggest challenges for you in terms of bringing UX to your team and to your clients?

Amy: Helping people understand what UX is: you're not just concerned with what this page says, it's how you're saying it and how that's reflected elsewhere in the site. It's how that user is going to go from here to here to here, and what they're going to expect when they click something.

Dani: Do you feel that there are any UX techniques that are particularly useful with Drupal over other technologies? Or do you find that the process is about the same?

Amy: Because I tend to break things up into pieces—site flows and personas, or pain points and that sort of thing—Drupal actually helps because it's very much an evolving product. If you're implementing a new module, for example, there are various pieces at play, so it's easier to explain to a client that they're not going to be able to see instant implementation, because there's so much more to it than just turning something on.

Drupal also helps create the expectation that a website is not a fixed thing. You get it out there, you mold it, and you shape it, and it changes as your needs and your strategy change. Drupal is very flexible and open, which makes it easier to drive that message home.

Dani: Even as a designer, there is a sort of re-education process once you get into Drupal. I came from the Wordpress world, and it felt like you would put up a blog, put up a few other pages, and then you were good to go. With Drupal, you had to get into that space where you were now talking about discrete sections of the site almost as a specific chunk of functionality. You really do have to, in order to engage a very rapid and iterative and, indeed, agile, process, understand that you can't have a project plan that says, "Okay, on the week of the 14th, we're going to do all of the content types for the site."

Amy (laughing): Exactly.

Dani: And I've seen project plans that were like that, where on the week of the 14th we were going to do all of the content types, and on the week of the 20th, we're going to do all the Views.

Amy: It's very integrated, so you can't break it up like you're used to doing traditionally —you know, "We're going to build something manually to update the content with PHP, so we can self-contain this little project and you don't ever have to think about the rest of the site." Drupal really forces you to think about the site holistically every time you do something.

Dani: You have to think about how things fit together, how content is organized, how it's formatted, because all of that feeds into your workflow.

Amy: Yes, because there's so many hooks in and out. From a user flow standpoint, it's great, because you can't really ever self-contain an area of the site. There's this need to keep it constantly in check—how the piece you're working on is impacting other areas of the site. That's fantastic from a UX standpoint. It does make managing pieces of a project much more complex, but it's a great self-check for managing that entire user experience, and managing it over time.

Dani: It's also good for establishing design patterns. There are ways that Views work out, and it's not because that's just what Earl decided to do after a couple of Mountain Dews, it's because this is the way it's supposed to look.

Amy: And you can reuse those things too. It lends itself to reusing components very easily, so you don't have to start from scratch every time you do something.

Dani: So what do you think of as your role in the Drupal community, or rather the role of UX in the Drupal community?

Amy: I see it as, for lack of a better word, advocacy. I'm not a coder. I don't know how many UX people, if they specialize in that, are coders by nature; our biggest role is getting out there and advocating for the use of the product: being able to articulate why it works and how it works and being that translator between the two worlds. And really pushing the product forward: getting people using it, and using it *well* so that the community can continue.

User Experience: Bringing UX Design to an embedded team

If you're a designer who wants to bring UX principles into your next project, whether it's for a small project or for a larger team with multiple stakeholders, here's some advice from my experience working with a variety of clients and design teams. If you find you're really interested in this stuff, check out the resources at the end of this chapter for a list of articles and books I've found useful.

Study the organization you're working with

Working in any kind of organization requires a certain taste for politics. As designers, we get this already; we're used to having our work critiqued, and dealing with comments that we find, *ahem*, unhelpful. The trick to selling stakeholders on user experience design is, like visual design, in understanding its value to the organization and being able to back that up with hard facts. Speaking the language of the client also helps. This is where documentation comes in especially handy. If you can point to a specific objective that your approach will help meet, you're well on your way to selling the idea.

Just as important as figuring out how to sell the idea of UX design to your clients is realizing when the client is a lost cause. In *Undercover User Experience Design* (New

Riders Press), authors Cennydd Bowles and James Box offer some important red flags to watch out for when broaching the subject of user experience:

1. **Design Disinterest**. "Many organizations simply don't care about design, or see it as an expensive luxury rather than a strategic investment."[*] We've all met clients like this; they might focus on engineering more than design, or they might focus on what their competitors are doing to the point where they become little more than a "me too" business. If you can convince them of the value of your approach, supplementing your work with case studies from similar organizations who have been successful with this approach, you can help them make the switch into a design-forward company.

2. **Cash Cows**. If the company has a certain product, or area of the site, that generates huge amounts of revenue, no matter how poorly designed, expect a fight when you suggest changes to them. If you're still trying to introduce the concept of UX design to the company, you're better off leaving these areas alone unless you can prove your work will have a positive effect on the revenue stream for that product.

3. **Enormous expectations and difficult deadlines**. "Sky-high expectations can cause disappointment, paralyzing fear of failure, and poor decisions."[†] Combining too-high expectations with unreasonable deadlines for delivery is a recipe for failure. If you run into this type of situation, the most important thing to do is understand what's underneath these expectations, and see if you can shift the focus towards something that's more reasonable. If stakeholders aren't willing to budge, it's time to move on.

In addition to these flags, it's important to look at the organizational structure and decision-making process within the company. How many stakeholders are you dealing with? What's the approval process like? Are there any places where you can find an easy win, or does it look like this will be a struggle from start to finish? In time, you'll get better at figuring out which clients you can help and which will be an uphill battle.

It's not about looks

This is a tricky subject, coming from the world of brand design as I (and many of you, presumably) do. But if there's one truth I must impress upon you, it is this: *user experience design is not about how something looks; it's about how it works.* Is good UX design pretty? Often, yes. But is pretty design good UX? You'd be surprised how often it isn't.

Good UX design must balance the needs of the person visiting the site with the business objectives of the client who owns the site. This means, in order to truly create good UX (and I've found this true of most design challenges), *you must be able to speak to the client's business goals, and to the path the user will need to take in order to help the client*

---

[*] Bowles and Box, *Undercover User Experience Design* (New Riders Press), p. 20.

[†] Ibid, p. 21.

achieve those goals. This often means that, in the beginning stages of a user-centered design process, aesthetic issues (colors, fonts, etc.) will take a backseat to more pragmatic issues of sensible layout, information architecture and functional requirements. It also might mean that you make visual compromises that you really aren't happy with, if it makes the user's job easier. Thankfully, this is rare—but it does, and will, happen.

Let go of the outcome

This, admittedly, is a lesson from my yoga practice—but it's also a valuable lesson from working with clients and development teams. One of the more interesting parts of UX Design for the web is that there are many clients who still don't understand what it means, or how it can help their business. As such, be prepared for stakeholders who will bring up strong objectives to the approach you're trying to take, or managers who say they don't want to "waste time" on personas, user flows, or other common tasks associated with UX work. Also, be prepared to meet a number of people who get UX and UI design confused, and think of UX as playing around with Fireworks and jQuery, with a bit of usability testing thrown in.

User Experience: Techniques for Drupal

One of the challenges inherent in doing UX work is knowing who's responsible for it. In some teams I've spoken to, it's the project manager's job to create many of the documents associated with UX (personas, site maps, wireframes); in others, there's a specific team member who's completely dedicated to user experience design for the project. The methods and documentation that you use will vary according to project as well. For some clients, you'll find yourself doing elaborate user personas and backing them up with weeks of research; for others, a quick and dirty approach—where you use existing information on customers to create a persona that you then test as you prototype—is more than appropriate. The point of UX documentation is *to always do some, but to only do the things that make sense for the project.*

Below are some methods that I've found helpful. Many of them are borrowed from traditional UX methodologies; however, most of them have been adapted in one way or another for my Drupal workflow. Over time, you'll find a method that works for you. If anything, the key to working with UX documentation is to find a balance between an efficient workflow for you and creating something that effectively communicates to the client.

Mind mapping

Mind mapping is a relatively quick and simple way to get a lot of ideas out on the table in one big brain dump, and take a high-level view to recognize the patterns. Whether you're doing the map in software or with pen and paper, the point of a mind-map is to generate as many ideas as you can related to a specific issue, then to step back and recognize the patterns that pop up (see Figure 2-1).

The times when I find mind-mapping most effective are when the objectives for a project are fuzzy or the client has trouble articulating them. By laying everything out in a visual format—either on a whiteboard or with a pile of post-its—you can often get the client to recognize their own patterns, or the deeper problems underneath the surface problem they're usually trying to solve. They're also very effective for outlining user characteristics; I use mind-maps often to find common threads in the clients I work with, for example, when I'm working on my marketing plan.

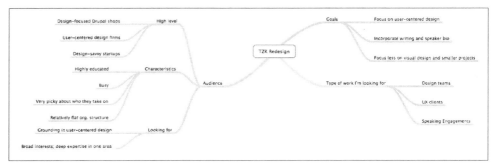

Figure 2-1. Mind maps can be a helpful way to quickly flesh out an idea for a site. The above is an initial map for my professional site redesign (in progress).

The best thing about mind maps is that they're quick; good software will often allow you to very quickly create and link thoughts to each other. In many cases, you can even create a mind map during a conversation with a client, and convert the result into a set of bullet points for a project plan. For computer-based maps, I like MindNode‡ for Mac, or MindJet Manager for PC/Mac§. MindNode's basic version is free, and has many of the basic features you might need for efficient mindmapping; MindManager is pricier, but I find the interface and templates much more efficient to work with.

‡ *http://www.mindnode.com/mindnode/professional/*

§ *http://www.mindjet.com/mindmanager-mac*

User personas

A good user persona describes a specific person who is visiting your site, and focuses on documenting specific tasks they want to achieve, and the reasons that people are visiting the site. Every team does it differently, but there are a few components that make a persona valuable in the design process:

- **They involve real data**. If you don't have actual interviews, talk to your client about their clients, and get some real data about how they want to interact with the site.
- **They help map functional or content areas of the site to specific needs the user has**. The point of a persona isn't to tell a nice story about Judy the housewife; it's to make sure that everything you're putting into a given site maps to a specific user need. This makes personas particularly valuable for working with stakeholders who tend to come up with long lists of requirements that aren't necessarily useful.
- **They help the design and production team understand what they need to build**. A set of well thought-out personas can clarify the overall direction for a site, answer questions about new things that come up, and keep the team on track.

For most sites, you will have anywhere from one to four personas for different user segments. For example, a simple corporate site might have a persona for their target customer, another for the media, and another for others in their industry. If your client has broken up their target customers into different market segments, you may have a persona for each of them, or use your personas to demonstrate the commonality among a set of market segments. Figure 2-2 shows a sample persona for a site for holistic moms.

When building personas, the important thing to remember is that your focus should be not on *who they are*, but on *what they're there to do*. For example, an online banking website could have any number of user types, ranging from 20-year-old college students to retirees. A persona for this application, then, would focus on specific user tasks, rather than age/income demographics. This is not only useful in the beginning of the project, when you're just getting into the topic of user research, it's even more useful later in the project, when you have to defend your design decisions to the client.

Judy A. Doe
Drupal Role: Authenticated
Client Market Segment: New Lead

"I want to raise my children the organic way."

User Priorities

- find relevant information quickly,
- learn from others in her position

Business Priorities

- collect e-mail address for partner promotions;
- get user to refer friends to the site

Relevant Functionality/ Content Areas

- Health and Wellness section;
- Content Search;
- User Forums

User Scenario

Judy is a stay-at-home mother with a 9-year-old daughter in Lexington, Massachusetts. She shops regularly at her local farmer's market, and is committed to raising her daughter on organic fruits and vegetables.

Recently, her daughter Lexi came down with an ear infection. The doctor prescribed her antibiotics, but she's concerned about giving them to her. She came to holisticmommies.org to see if any other organic-minded mothers have found a natural solution to ear infections

Figure 2-2. A sample persona. Note that it points to content/functionality this user might find especially useful. This is a great way to show stakeholders which functionality to prioritize—which is especially useful if they're trying to prioritize functionality that's expensive to build and not terribly useful to anyone visiting the site.

From the Trenches: Richard Banfield, Fresh Tilled Soil

Fresh Tilled Soil is a UI firm based in Waltham, MA that specializes in high-end application and UI design for startups. Richard Banfield, CEO of Fresh Tilled, is a proponent of the Lean Startup methodology. In the Lean world, similar to Agile, design starts with a set of user stories and behavior flows, put together quickly as hypotheses to test in the real world.

Dani: One of the things that we talked about was that you don't like personas.

Richard: It's not that I don't like personas. It's that personas do not solve the UI/UX problem. A persona is an opportunity to take those visions you have about who your audience is and test it against some kind of model. Let's understand that better so we can build a better product. What it doesn't do, and what my fear about using personas only comes out of is: Where's the horizontal behavior?

I can show you a 23-year-old using a particular application. So—young, female, urban, tech savvy, using an application—and then I'll show you a 65-year-old immigrant using that same application, who's not tech savvy, who's on a completely different demographic spectrum. Where's the persona there? No longer is it Jane the persona; now it's a set of behaviors.

Dani: For me, documentation was always two things. First, it was framing the design challenge, and really understanding what we were doing here. Second, it was a way for me to point to something when the client started coming to me with every random objection you can think of.

Richard: Right—keeps them focused.

Dani: How do you keep the client focused on the right topic? How do you keep the ship going in the right direction?

Richard: Let's think about all the documentation. There's the Scope of Work, which tells the client what you've agreed to do with them. (And any change to that must be accompanied by a Change Order. This is kind of litigious stuff, or basic project management.) The Scope of Work may also include the development of personas, or the development of behavioral paths or flows.

Beyond the Scope of Work is the schedule: what is it that we can achieve. That's driven, in our world, somewhat by Agile, mostly by Lean, and that's about the Minimum Viable Product by a certain date. So the client says, "I want to launch on the 25th of June." You say, "What can be done in that time?" and, "What can be done that's going to move the needle?" Beyond that, it's, "What are the flows that need to happen in the construct of this website that will allow us to achieve the behavioral goals that we need to achieve for this particular set of audience members?"

It's not that we don't consider personas, not to say that personas are irrelevant, but what you have to do is make sure that if you are going to talk about those personas, you understand what behavior is associated with that persona, and is that behavior horizontally achievable across lots of different personas?

I'll give you a good example: People do things for two reasons: because it's *easy*, and because they're *motivated*. A one-step shopping cart, like Amazon has, is easy. So even if you don't have high motivation to buy that new chair, or that new item of clothing, it's so easy to do that you might as well do it. Then there's the motivational sell; there's fear, and love, and all the other emotions that come into it.

What we've discovered, mostly through studying the work of people like BJ Fogg and other behaviorists, is that when you construct a flow you need to do *easy* first, *motivation* second. It's kind of like this reverse pattern where, by making something easy to do, you increase motivation, and by increasing motivation you make it continually easier to do.

Our documentation (or our delivery document) could outline four or five different flows: Here's what happens when this person is just browsing the internet and comes across you; here's what happens when they see your display banner; here's what happens when they're referred by a friend; here's what happens when they see you, but don't come back for six months and then come back again. Now *that* worries less about the persona, and more about the behavior.

We found this out the hard way. We work with a company called Perk Street Financial. When they first launched, they literally had cardboard cutouts. They said, "This is our persona." It was a tech-savvy, young, urban individual who wants a debit card with rewards. We designed a site for that, and the site we designed wasn't incorrect, but the message that we gave the marketers was incorrect, because they then went out and marketed to tech-savvy young urbanites. It turns out that their audience was actually married families with 2.5 kids who are Evangelistic Midwesterners. You can't get two more extreme personas. And their behavior is different.

Designers no longer have the luxury of saying, "I designed it; it looks good; I achieved all the goals set out in the design process—now it's your turn to make it successful by marketing and selling it." No amount of marketing or sales dollars is going to change the fact that it doesn't resonate with that audience.

User Flows

User Flows are very similar to user scenarios, with the exception of format; while a scenario tends to focus on prose, a user flow is a visual framework that describes the specific journey a user takes from point A to point B. For example, say you want to understand (or describe to a client) the decision process a user might take for creating an account. What's their incentive? How do they make the decision? What are the intermediate steps? A user flow can help you walk the client (or yourself) through the process visually.

I often find user flows most helpful when framing a specific design challenge; for example, how a user might decide to make a purchase, or what would lead a person to sign up for an account. The important thing to remember about any type of flow is that they're often more useful for you than they are to the client; if you do decide to present them to the client, make sure it's in the context of making sure you understand the design challenge, and not as presenting a possible solution.

Similar to Mind Maps and other visually oriented documents, I tend to start my user flows with pencil and paper (Figure 2-3), and gradually move them into a program such as OmniGraffle or Keynote (Figure 2-4).

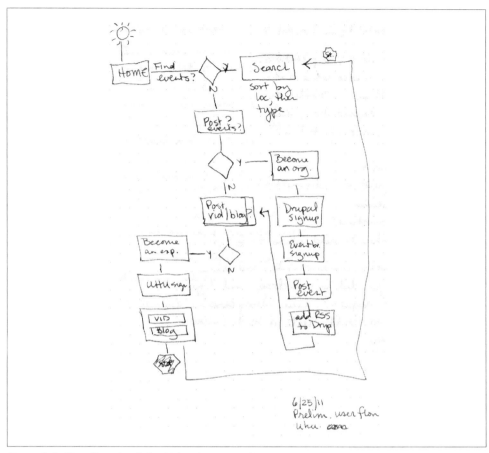

Figure 2-3. User flow sketch for Urban Homesteaders Unite.

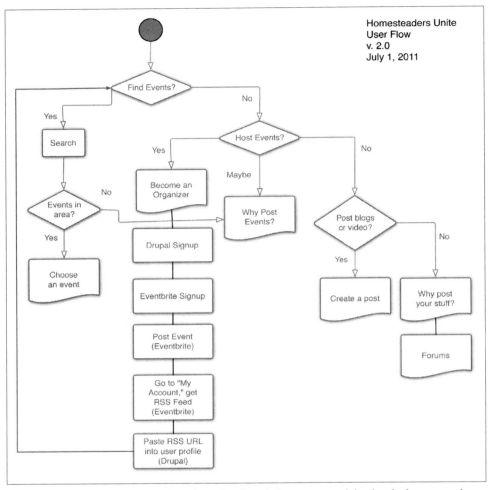

Figure 2-4. Version 2 of the same flow, formalized. Both this version and the sketch above were shown to and discussed with the design team.

Functional Breakdowns

A functional breakdown is about what it sounds like: it breaks down the functionality that you're creating into manageable chunks. For simple sites, this could be sections of content, such as the blog, or the events page; for more complex sites, this could be the shopping cart, or a particular widget. The key to functional breakdowns is breaking up the site's implementation into chunks that are easy for stakeholders to recognize and your team to focus on at once. It also helps with identifying Minimum Viable Product, a fancy Agile/Lean programming term that means "the most basic level of functionality that will still be relevant to the user's goals."

It's important to note, as Todd Nienkerk of Austin's Four Kitchens has pointed out to me, that Minimum Viable Product is less about trying to work less, and more about giving clients a return on their investment by getting them usable code as quickly as possible. This approach also has significant benefits for strategic UX; getting useable code into the world more quickly gives you a better opportunity to have real users interacting with your site quickly. This gives you valuable data that will help you continually improve the user experience of your site.

With Drupal, this concept becomes especially important; setting your bar for Minimum Viable Product too high can lead to exceptionally long development cycles which drive clients crazy; setting it too low can result in a site that always looks half-finished.

When I do a functional breakdown, I like to do it in spreadsheet form, often a Google Doc (or Excel, if there are data security issues around the project) and list sub-tasks underneath the larger banner. For example, on a very simple site, a functional breakdown might start like this:

1. Major Pages
   - About Us
   - Contact Form
   - Services
   - Testimonials
2. Blog
   - Content received
   - Content Types created
   - Views displays created
   - Content entered and tagged

On top of these basic tasks, I'll often map functionality to its relevance for specific user personas/scenarios that we've identified, and for the complexity it will require to build. This is especially helpful for more complex implementations; if your client wants a component that's going to be especially tricky to build, but your user research indicates that their users don't really find it valuable to their activities on the site, seeing the contrast between user needs and the resources required to build non-essential functionality can often help clients re-prioritize in your favor.

Screen Sketches and Wireframes

Screen sketches can be created in Fireworks, Omnigraffle or any other software of your choosing; however, for me, they always start with pencil and paper. The point to starting with paper is the flexibility; when you're first ideating a web interface, quantity is much more important than quality. My initial sketches, done in pencil, are a mess more often than not. I use them primarily to work out issues of content placement, calls to action, and other basic "why are we here?" issues. As the ideas get refined, and things start making sense, the sketches (still in pencil) start getting more refined as well, and eventually I can put them into a format that makes sense to someone who isn't me.

We'll get deeper into Wireframes in the *Design and Prototyping* guide, including some of the different methodology and tricks that the Drupal community has come up with for creating effective wireframes and visual layouts.

Wireflows

Wireflows are similar to a user flow in the sense that they map out a user's journey from point A to point B, but instead of simple directives (Build a Product, Create an Account, etc.) they show sample screens that the user would visit on their way to their destination.

Wireflows are especially useful for complex applications that require the collection of user data; for example, a shopping cart or a user registration screen. Rather than trying to wireframe each individual screen in Fireworks, and explain them to stakeholders as individual pages, you can walk them through the entire flow and show them the information you're collecting as you walk through the flow. This not only speeds up the stakeholder feedback process, but it gives you an opportunity to map out potential interface challenges in a way that you often can't working with individual screens. If using wireflows, it's important to manage expectations carefully; as a necessarily low-fi prototype, they can confuse clients who are expecting more high-fidelity deliverables.

Content Strategy Documents

Content strategy document can be anything from an inventory of current content to an in-depth analysis of content types, user roles, and a comprehensive site map. Since working with content can be one of the most complex and time-consuming pieces of working with Drupal (no, really), it's vital that you take time to understand the actual content you're working with, and how it all fits together in the user experience.

UX Techniques and Drupal: Practical issues to hammer out

Most of the techniques I've laid out here could work for any web project. How, you might be asking, would they be different in Drupal?

The main differences you'll see working with these documents in Drupal is the pieces of the design puzzle you're building, and how they fit together. The Drupal framework has certain things baked into it—for example, the concept of Views or Blocks—and these can inform many of your deliverables in ways that aren't necessarily true for other implementations. At the same time, it's important to remember that the purpose of deliverables is to communicate; while your developers would probably understand intuitively that content on a particular wireframe would be coming from some Drupal module or field, inserting this logic into client-facing deliverables can cause confusion.

For this reason, many designers have developed a layered approach to client-facing UX deliverables. In a persona, for example, you might include the user's Drupal role (which determines the permissions they have on your site) under their name, but you might also include the user's assumed market segment to help the client understand who the persona represents. In a wireframe, you might stick to a more basic boxes-and-labels approach for showing the client, but you might have a separate "annotations" layer that shows the implementation team where specific content is coming from within Drupal.

The *Design and Prototyping* guide offers a number of these types of adaptations, and also includes links to several Drupal-specific templates that the community has developed for commonly used applications.

Go Deeper: User Experience and Project Management

Books

- Bowles, Cannydd and Box, James. (2011) *Undercover User Experience: Learn how to do great UX work with tiny budgets, no time, and limited support.* New York, NY: New Riders Press.
- Brown, Dan. (2006) *Communicating Design*, Second Edition. New York, NY: New Riders Press.
- Krug, Steve. (2005) *Don't Make Me Think: A common sense approach to web usability*, Second Edition. New York, NY: New Riders Press.
- Brown, Sunni, Dave Gray and James Macanufo. (2010) *Gamestorming: A playbook for innovators, rulebreakers, and changemakers.* New York, NY: O'Reilly Media.
- Norman, Don. (2011) *Living with Complexity.* Cambridge, MA: MIT Press.

Websites

52 weeks of UX. A blog about the process of designing for real people, published weekly. *http://52weeksofux.com.*

UX Magazine. A constantly updated magazine about varied topics of user experience design. *http://uxmag.com.*

UX Matters. Another online magazine about user experience, although not as pretty as UX Magazine. *http://uxmatters.com.*

CHAPTER 3

Fleshing Things Out:
Getting ready to prototype

This chapter deals with some practical issues of planning a Drupal implementation. In the first section, *Working with Content*, we'll discuss why it's vital to start working with real content right away in your Drupal site. In the second, *Choosing Modules*, we talk about the process of selecting the right modules for your site. There's also an entirely non-comprehensive list of contributed modules that you might find Very Useful.

Working with content

In the Old Days™, building a promotional website was a fairly straightforward affair. You'd go through a discovery process, create a couple of wireframes—generally for the home page and 1-2 interior pages, then mock up and iterate designs. When those designs were approved by the client, you'd whip up a fancy template in HTML and start laying in the content and images.

Content, almost always, came later. You'd have a sense of the site map, and how it might evolve—you needed that for navigation—but the actual content was rarely something you saw in the early phases of developing wireframes. Generally, this wasn't a problem; as you were coding the content by hand within the template, you could adjust the template relatively easily once you had content to work with.

With Drupal, as with many other content management systems, things aren't that easy. Some elements will be familiar, especially if you've gotten used to systems like Wordpress. At the most basic level, you're dealing with a series of page templates, and those templates put your content into specific areas of the page. You style those templates in your theme layer, and that makes the page look good.

What makes Drupal complex, but also terrific, is the amount of control you have over almost every aspect of the site's pages. The key to making sense of this complexity is to understand that *each page of a Drupal website is a collection of different pieces of content that are located within your site's database and files.* Because of Drupal's inherent flexibility, that content can be organized and formatted in any number of different ways —and it will need to be, in order to finish the project with a working site.

For this reason, I've found that two things are essential to getting started on any Drupal project:

1. *Shifting the way that you think about page layout for the web.* You're not looking at it in terms of generic page grids anymore (although that's certainly a component of it). To actually succeed in creating a Drupal site, you need the ability to think of a page layout in terms of the organization of information on the page. What will the content be? What are the different sections you'll need, and how will they be organized on the page? How will the content be found or searched for—in top level navigation, by browsing categories, or some other way? Visual design is an important component of that, but it should always come after this first issue has been dealt with.

2. As a way of reinforcing #1, *every Drupal project should start with 1–3 samples of actual content that will appear on the actual site.*

Over the years, I've seen some resistance to this concept—developers, for example, like to think in terms of building things quickly, and clients can have a hard time grasping the idea that they need to be able to provide content before they see page layouts. But there's a very specific reason for this need. As mentioned above, every page of your Drupal site is constructed from different bits of content that are stored in different locations in the system, and then collected onto the page. This means, in order to construct the actual pages, you need to start loading actual content into the system as soon as you can.

Drupal works by organizing content into different *content types* (see Chapter 1 if you need a definition of what a content type is). It also allows you to add and display as many custom fields on those content types as you can (which is very useful for making content look the way you want it to on the page). This flexibility is one of the key reasons it is imperative to work with actual content instead of placeholder text. Seeing the content allows you to visualize its fundamental components, and allows you to set some formatting parameters that will protect the client's content strategy after they take over management of the site.

The layout of a Drupal page can be constructed from any number of things:

1. Actual node content (remember, Drupal calls content *nodes*);
2. Views displays that organize several nodes together.
3. Blocks that can be created either with custom text/HTML or as Views displays.
4. Menus that can be created in any number of ways.
5. Custom code built into the page template.

For example, a standard events page on a corporate website would likely consist of the following (see Figure 3-1):

1. An "event" content type, with a Title, Description, Date, and Link to an external website or registration page.
2. A View called "events" which would list all events in chronological order.
3. Displays based on the "events" View that would show as a block of titles and dates for the home page, an Events archive (showing events that have passed) and an "Upcoming Events" page (showing events that haven't happened yet).

Figure 3-1. The events page of alberieco.com (http://alberieco.com). Design by the zen kitchen.

In addition to these, you might have categories for different types of events, links to external resources (such as a book to read or a packing list), and any other permutation of the Event content type your clients can come up with. Starting the process with dummy content only gets you so far; if the live content will be different than what you're assuming, you'll find yourself with a load of headaches before you know it.

Trial by fire

My first major Drupal site was for a small business owner in the Boston area. In our initial discussions, we'd talked about doing a simple refresh of her existing site, and I sold her on the idea of doing it in Drupal. We discussed the site map, and the way that content was going to be organized, but she hadn't developed any of the new content yet. As was my process at the time, I worked up a proposed layout for the homepage and an interior page, and she approved it with no problems. Look and feel established, I started up an installation of Drupal and started creating the content types that would organize the site's content, working with generic placeholder text.

The site map we'd originally agreed on was fairly simple:

1. A Services page that listed all the services her company offered;
2. An Events page that listed upcoming events (this would require an *event* content type)
3. A News page that listed current news (this would require a *news* content type)
4. An About page that listed all the staff and what they brought to the company;
5. A Resources page that listed resources for her clients;
6. A contact form that would allow users to get in touch with her for consultations.

All of this seemed pretty straightforward. When the content started coming in, it turned out that the Services page was actually several different services, each with fourteen pages of descriptive content. The staff bios were two pages long. Events could be categorized, and had to be navigated, in three separate ways. And the landing pages for each of these content sections should only show teaser content (i.e. a picture, title that links to the full content, and an intro paragraph). Most of her requests made perfect sense, but none of them had been discussed in our discovery sessions, nor were they reflected in the designs that had been comped and approved. Eventually, I had to re-do all the work that had already been done, which threw the project into massive delays.

From that point on, I made it part of my discovery process to get actual content from the client before I start working with Drupal on any project. While this policy isn't without its challenges, it has resulted in a much more efficient workflow over the years. This is especially true for large, complex sites—but as with the previous example, it can even be true of smaller sites.

Working with Content Types: a High-Level Overview

As mentioned previously, Drupal works by separating content into distinct content types. The best way to determine which content types your site will need is through the site map and wireframes that were done in the UX/discovery phase. Site maps and high-level navigation items will guide you in creating content types, while wireframes and site designs offer insight into the types of content you need to accommodate (text, images, video, etc.), what special fields you might have to create, and how those fields should be formatted (see Figure 3-3).

If you (or someone on your team) developed a site map during the Discovery or UX phase, you can work directly with the site map to determine content types. Working with a printout, or in a program like OmniGraffle, start marking up the site map with notes (see Figure 3-2). These notes should include possible fields you might need, categories users might expect for the content, and other questions that arise from the site map. For example: do we want to have testimonials from clients? Should those appear as a block on several pages, or just as a page? How are we organizing news items? How many authors will be on the blog? Etc. This will help you get oriented, and you can better communicate to the client and the team what the content needs will be.

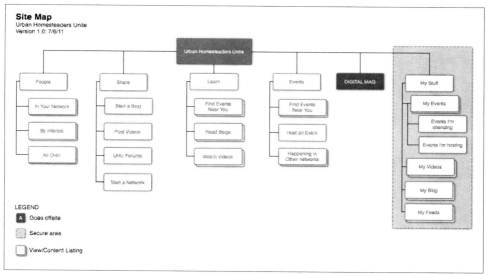

Figure 3-2. A site map can give you a head start on which content types you'll need. This site map notes with double boxes which content pages will be coming from Views; each of those types of content lists could be its own content type, e.g., Blog Entries, Videos, Events, etc.

When you have sample content from the client, print out the content file (double-sided) and start writing on it. Note extra fields, taxonomy categories you'll have to create, and how to break up the content on the landing pages for that section. If wireframes or site designs have already been created, be sure to check them against the content you've received; you'd be surprised how often they differ.

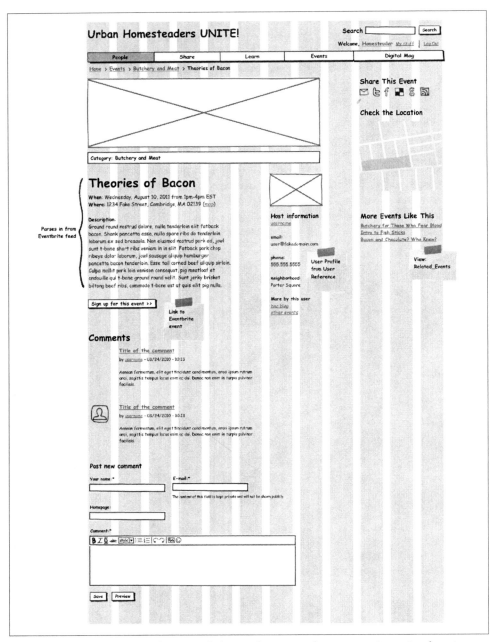

Figure 3-3. Annotating a wireframe can help you figure out where content is coming from in your Drupal site. In this mockup for a project in process, most of the page information is coming in (ideally) from an Eventbrite feed.

The number of extra fields you include in a content type will vary; I've had projects where every content type was basically a title, description and image, and I've had projects where every content type required anywhere from 5–30 extra fields, each of which had to be formatted and displayed in a certain way based on what situation the user was in at the time they were viewing it. This, if you haven't guessed yet, is why you need the content FIRST—if you think you're doing the former, and find out you're doing the latter, your life will be very, very bad while you switch gears.

Once you've sketched out an overview of what you're really looking at, and confirmed these assumptions with the client, it's time to start creating the content types themselves. Building out content types can be one of the most time intensive pieces of creating a Drupal site if the content types you're working with are very complex.

First you start creating fields, then re-order them if you need to, change the way they're displayed (do they need the field label? Should it be above the content or in line with it? Do you even need to show the field? Do we want to group them a certain way?), and create a single piece of content to test that it looks right on the page. For a very simple content type (most News content types, or Basic Page content types, for example), this can take a few minutes. For more complex content types (such as a Product description, or a content type that maps to several pieces of related content), this back and forth can take days.

Because this chapter is focused on planning and managing a project, we won't get into the process of how to create content types; if you have never done it before, check out the following resources on creating content types in Drupal 7:

> *http://www.youtube.com/watch?v=iibPX5KBFu4*: A video demonstration of creating content types.
> *http://yadadrop.com/drupal-video/drupal-7-creating-content-types*: Another video tutorial.

Also, check out the next chapter, *Choosing Modules*, for some modules that can help with content types and custom fields.

Organizing your content

Setting up content types is one piece of the content puzzle. Once you've gotten the content types somewhat organized, and sample content into the site, you want to start putting them into Views displays. I, like many of my Drupal brethren, have a love/hate relationship with Views. On one hand, Views is an incredibly powerful tool for getting content to display in any possible combination you can think of. This makes it easier to build massively complex sites while keeping them relatively easy to maintain. On the other hand, Views is so complex that even the most seasoned developers occasionally can't make heads or tails of it.

For the designer, or even the solo site builder, it's useful to have the basics down when it comes to Views. While the first few Views you create will always leave you grinding your teeth, it's actually relatively easy to put them together once you get the system down. Additionally, Views allows you to clone views and individual displays, which makes it much easier to create additional views once you have the first one finished. For the purposes of this chapter, we're only going to discuss how to figure out which Views you'll need, and how they should be displayed.

To figure out which Views you need, start with your site map and any wireframes that have been created in the design process. Anything that looks like a list of content, titles, or links to content, is most likely going to require a View. Sample views might include:

- A menu of recent blog entries for the sidebar of each page;
- A menu of categories for a specific type of content;
- A News page or Events calendar;
- A staff directory or list of bios;
- A list of blog posts related to the one a user is reading;
- A jQuery slideshow of featured content on the home page;
- A single entry from the blog that appears in the site's footer or in a promotional area on the homepage.

All of these things can be created with Views.

By default, Views allows you to create the following displays:

- Pages (i.e., A full page of content, which appears in the site's navigation);
- Blocks (i.e., A small block of content, which can appear anywhere on the site that you want it to)
- Attachments (i.e., A View with slightly different parameters that's attached to another View. This is useful, for example, if you want to display both Upcoming events and Recent events on the same page)
- RSS Feeds.

Each of these displays can be output in a variety of formats, including an HTML list (good for building sidebar menus or lists of related content), an unformatted list (the default display, good for displaying content on a page), tables and multi-column grids. Adding a few handy contributed modules can open up more possibilities for formatting your Views displays:

- JQuery slideshows. These are particularly helpful for creating featured content, or for highlighting specific projects or products. My favorite slideshow module is Views Slideshow (drupal.org/project/views_slideshow (*http://drupal.org/project/ views_slideshow*)). While it has its limitations and dependencies, it's the most reliable of the slideshow modules I've seen.
- Calendars of Events, or pages that have time-sensitive content. This is where the Date module (drupal.org/project/date (*http://drupal.org/project/date*)) comes in handy. The Date module comes with a sub-module called Date Views; *you will*

need to enable this module in order to get Views to work correctly on anything that involves a date.

- All manner of JQuery effects: accordions, sliders, and anything you can think of. While it is often advisable to build these things into your theme manually, there are many contributed modules available that can create the formatting for you. Just be aware that they (and Views Slideshow, for that matter) often don't create the prettiest code.

Again, since we're focusing on content strategy here and less on Drupal implementation, we won't get into how to create Views in this book. However, there are quite a few excellent video tutorials that you can check out if you haven't played with Views yet:

http://lin-clark.com/blog/intro-drupal-7-intro-views-pt-1: Intro to Views, by Lin Clark (just ignore the Drush stuff).

http://www.metaltoad.com/Drupal-7-Tutorial-Creating-Edit-Content-Links -Views: a Very Comprehensive tutorial from Dan Linn at Metal Toad Media on creating "edit content" links using Views. It also gives a quick overview of the new Views interface, which is a massive improvement over the last version.

http://nodeone.se/blogg/learn-views-screencast-series-summed-up: an entire set of Drupal videos that walk through the Views process in a variety of contexts, by NodeOne in Stockholm, Sweden. I cannot recommend these videos highly enough.

Putting this all together

In theory, each member of the team will be dealing with its own piece of this giant puzzle called building a website. In practice, especially on small teams, you'll often find yourself switching back and forth among different phases of the content development cycle. A typical Drupal project, for example, might look like this:

1. Site map and wireframes are created and approved;
2. The designer (you) starts adding in visual elements;
3. The front-end developer (or you) starts creating content types and fields;
4. Site content comes in, and looks different from the wireframes and designs that have been approved;
5. The front-end developer (or you) goes back and starts changing content types, fields, views, etc. to mesh with the content files;
6. The client decides that the content should be changed to match the designs;
7. The front-end developer (or you) goes back and starts changing content types, fields, views, etc. BACK to where they were before;
8. And so on, and so on...

Somewhere in this whole mess, theming also has to happen. In larger teams, the designer will often work directly with a front-end developer to iterate designs and incorporate them into the site's theme. For smaller jobs, or solo gigs, you're the one doing the lion's share of the design, theming and content management. With time, you become used to it. A typical theming session for me usually involves tweaking the display of a field in my content type, then tweaking a display setting in one of the Views I created, then going back into CSS and making adjustments to that field's properties—in infinite combinations.

This is the single most important reason why it's important to get actual content as soon as you possibly can. The more you can allow the content to inform your designs, the fewer headaches you'll have in the design and development process. Your team will thank you, your client will love you, and your head will definitely thank you.

Choosing modules

Modules are one of the things that make Drupal terrific; however, they're also one of the things that makes Drupal frustrating to many people who are just discovering it. Knowing which module to choose, or which one is needed for a specific project, can be a challenge. And sometimes, a module that seems to be exactly what you need will end up causing more trouble than it fixes—either through refusing to play nice with other modules that you've installed, or through messy code that causes major cross-browser issues (hello, Facebook Social Plugins).

That said, there are many modules that are incredibly useful when working with Drupal. Some, such as Block Class (drupal.org/project/block_class (*http://drupal.org/project/block_class*)) and Pathauto/Token (drupal.org/project/pathauto (*http://drupal.org/project/pathauto*); drupal.org/project/token (*http://drupal.org/project/token*)) are so useful that I install them by default on any new installation. Others, such as View Reference (drupal.org/project/view_reference (*http://drupal.org/project/view_reference*)), I install whenever I need that specific functionality.

So many modules. How do I choose?

There's no specific science to choosing the right Drupal module for a given project. However, the more sites you build, the more you'll begin to notice that specific modules become common for a given project. As you experiment, you'll also get better at weeding out the modules that aren't terribly good from the ones that are rock solid. Some things to keep in mind when choosing modules for your project:

- **When possible, fewer modules is generally better**. Bear in mind that every module you enable on a Drupal site adds code and other things that the site needs to deal with in order to load the site. More things to deal with, the longer it takes for pages to load.

- **Look for modules that are actively maintained**. Each module's project page lists whether it's actively maintained, how long ago the code was updated, and the date of the last release. In general, it's best to choose modules that are listed as "Actively Maintained" and have a recommended release date within the last six months. Figure 3-4 shows an example of an actively maintained Drupal module.

- **If all else fails, reach out**. Can't figure out what you're looking for? Can't find the right module for your specific functional needs? A good developer can often help you create custom functionality (and is worth every penny you spend). Often, you can find advice and support from the Drupal community just by asking at a community event or online. Searching on Drupal.org (*http://drupal.org*) for "[list functionality here]" can also help find things you may not have thought to look for. Either way, don't worry; we've all been there.

The next section presents an entirely incomplete and unscientific list of some of my favorite Drupal 7 modules.

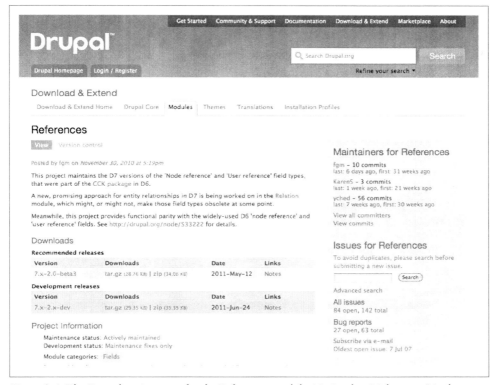

Figure 3-4. The Drupal project page for the References module. Notice that "6 days ago" in the upper right corner? That's a good thing.

Go-to modules

The following modules have a home in almost every Drupal project that I've done for the last three or four years. Some of them provide basic, common-sense functionality that's not available in Drupal core; others make theming or working with content easier.

Pathauto (drupal.org/project/pathauto (*http://drupal.org/project/pathauto*))

Pathauto helps you automatically create custom URLs for your site's pages. By default, Drupal will name every new piece of content *node/45* or something similar (the number represents the unique ID of the node). This is not only bad for SEO, but it's particularly bad for findability as your site grows in size. With Pathauto, Drupal will use the Title of the node as a default URL, making things much cleaner. You can also configure the settings to give specific content types their own prefix; for example, blog pages can have the custom URL *blog/[title]* as their URL. Pathauto requires the Token module (drupal.org/project/token (*http://drupal.org/project/token*)) to work properly.

Views (drupal.org/project/views (*http://drupal.org/project/views*))

Views, in its simplest form, is a database query. It's one of the most powerful contributed Drupal modules, and presents some of the biggest learning curves, even to people who use it for years. Once you get used to it, however, you can use it to create almost anything on a Drupal site—from a simple list of blog entries to dynamic menus to (with some help from different modules) clickable calendars and funky JQuery widgets. Recent updates to Views with Drupal 7 have made it much easier to get started working with Views; while there's still a significant learning curve, it's much easier to cross. As mentioned earlier, Swedish Drupal shop NodeOne did a terrific series of videos on learning Views in Drupal 7. Check out *http://nodeone.se/blogg/learn-views-screencast -series-summed-up* for a whole lot of Views love.

Block Class (drupal.org/block_class (*http://drupal.org/block_class*))

Once you get into theming Drupal sites, you notice a particular issue that happens. As you may recall from the introduction to DrupalSpeak™, Drupal constructs pages from a combination of Node content, Block content and occasionally Views displays. So let's say you have a menu in the sidebar of your page, as shown in Figure 3-5.

Figure 3-5. A simple menu of event categories.

If you were coding this in HTML, you'd create a `<div>` that would hold the menu, which is built as a `<ul>`, give it a class of *menu* or something similar, and then use CSS to style the menu.

Core Drupal behavior, however, doesn't make it so easy. Each block has a unique ID, but that ID usually has no relevance to what the block actually is. So, rather than having a block called "menu," you're searching for a block with an ID of *block-block-14* or something similar (Figure 3-6). So much fun, right?

```
▼<div class="region-inner region-sidebar-second-inner">
  ▼<section class="block block-views  contextual-links-region block-event-categories-block-1 block-views-event-categories-block-1
    odd" id="block-views-event-categories-block-1">
    ▼<div class="block-inner clearfix">
        <h2 class="block-title">Events by Category</h2>
      ►<div class="contextual-links-wrapper contextual-links-processed">…</div>
      ►<div class="content clearfix">…</div>
      </div>
    </section>
  </div>
```

Figure 3-6. Inspecting the element to find out how to style our block. What now?

Block class gives you the simple ability to assign classes to any block on the page, through the Block Configuration page (Figure 3-7).

Home » Administration » Structure » Blocks

▼ BLOCK CLASS SETTINGS

Customize the styling of this block by adding CSS classes. You can add multiple classes. IMPORTANT: You must add `<?php print $block_classes; ?>` to your theme's block.tpl.php file to make the classes appear. See the module's README.txt for more details.

CSS class(es)

event-categories

Separate classes with a space.

Figure 3-7. Adding a class to our block. Now we know what to call it in our CSS.

Not only is this useful for, say, establishing a common style for all sidebar menus on a given page, but if you're using a grid system such as 960.gs, you can assign grid values directly to blocks. This means that, rather than having to do a bunch of fancy tricks in your theme in order to accommodate a layout with blocks of multiple sizes, you can just give one block a class of "grid-4," another a class of "grid-6," and let the two float together in one region. We'll talk more about Grid Systems in the *Design and Prototyping* guide; in the meantime, check out 960.gs for an overview of the 960 Grid System, and you can also check out drupal.org/project/ninesixty (*http://drupal.org/project/ninesixty*) for the NineSixty base theme—or, if you're into responsive design, check out the Omega theme (drupal.org/project/omega), which has 960.gs built into a lovely responsive grid.

Webform (drupal.org/project/webform (*http://drupal.org/project/webform*))

Webform is a module that allows you to create custom forms (say, a contact form or a questionnaire) for your website. While Drupal comes with a contact form module directly in core, its functionality is limited to sending fairly simple e-mails to individual users on the site. Webform gives you not only the opportunity to customize your contact form's content, but also to customize who receives the various e-mails it generates. You can also use it to create custom surveys, which can be very useful for doing user research.

WYSIWYG (drupal.org/project/wysiwyg (*http://drupal.org/project/wysiwyg*))

Many Drupal developers (and even some designers) insist that they never use WYSIWYG editors. I'm not one of them. For one thing, clients expect them. We're accustomed to using them whenever we have to write something that's more than a sentence long—and the first time you leave one out of a site, you can guarantee that your client will ask you where it is.

WYSIWYG depends on the Libraries module (drupal.org/project/libraries (*http://drupal.org/project/libraries*)) in order to work; you'll also need to download an editor library from the web. The configuration page for the module will give links to different library; the one that I find works best (or, at least, sucks least) is the TinyMCE library.

Mollom (drupal.org/project/mollom (*http://drupal.org/project/mollom*))

Mollom is a service created by Dries Buytaert, Drupal's creator, that helps block and trap spam on your site. To use the module, you have to set up a free account on Mollom.com (*http://mollom.com*), register the URL of your website for tracking, and copy your public and private API keys (given to you by the Mollom site when you register the URL) into the Mollom settings page (yoursite.com/admin/config/content/mollom/settings (*http://yoursite.com/admin/config/content/mollom/settings*)). The Mollom service is free for smaller personal and small business/non-profit sites; larger sites may require signing up for a paid subscription.

Oh-So-Nice to Have Modules

While the modules listed above will prove useful on almost any site you build, the following modules are one that should at least make it onto your "I might need this for something" list.

Field Group (drupal.org/project/field_group (*http://drupal.org/project/field_group*))

Field Group gives you the ability to create groups of fields within Drupal. For example, let's say that you're creating an address book, and you want to separate the mailing address from e-mail/phone contact information. Using Field Group, you could display both sets of information in different groups, and theme them differently within your site. Field Groups can also be displayed as Vertical Tabs or Horizontal Tabs by configuring the Manage Display settings in your content type; this is very useful for dealing with complex content types that have a lot of fields.

Link (drupal.org/project/link (*http://drupal.org/project/link*))

Link helps you create a Drupal field formatted as a link.

Media (drupal.org/project/media (*http://drupal.org/project/media*))

Media helps you organize and store media (like audio and video) on a Drupal site. As of this writing, implementation is still a bit buggy, but it's still a useful module to have, especially if you want to host video or documents on your site.

References (drupal.org/project/references (*http://drupal.org/project/references*))

References gives you the ability to format Drupal fields as references to other content - such as nodes, user profiles, or taxonomy terms. This is useful if you want to show the author of a post, or related content for an article.

View Reference (drupal.org/project/viewreference (*http://drupal.org/project/viewreference*))

The References module, as you saw above, made it possible to reference a specific node or user within a field in your Drupal page—which is useful if you have related information to share after a blog post. But what if you want to show a bunch of related content, with some teaser information and an image? You could use Node reference, and format the display of the field to show the content's Teaser display rather than just titles; however, doing this causes Drupal to create a bunch of extra code that will slow down your site. Using Views reference, you can create a view that contains only the fields you want to display, formatted the way that you want to show them, and reference that View directly in a custom field.

Block Reference (drupal.org/project/block_reference (*http://drupal.org/project/block_reference*))

Normally, to place a block on a page, you'd use the Block configuration screen to place it inside a region, and customize which pages or content types it belonged on. Block Reference, while it doesn't replace this process, gives you the ability to reference a Drupal Block directly in a field. This is useful:

- When you want to place a block on only one page;
- When you want to place a block within the Content region in a particular location (say, within a field group, or underneath a description)

Block Reference doesn't replace the Block configuration screen for all blocks; menus, for example, still work best when you use the Block configuration screen to place them. But for highly specific blocks that need to show up within a node's content, this is an incredibly useful module.

Submitagain (drupal.org/project/submitagain (*http://drupal.org/project/submitagain*))

Submitagain is a deceptively simple, but incredibly useful, module. What it does is allows you to create a setting when you're creating a content type—through a simple checkbox on the content type edit form—that will give you an option to "Save & Add Another" when you create a piece of that type of content.

Why is this wonderful? Let's say you're doing an online directory of association members for your local trade group. You likely have a list of folks with name, address, and other contact information to enter into the site. Normally, you'd have to choose *Add Content > Member* (assuming that you're working with a content type called "Member") for each time you create a new Member. With this module, you'd be able to add a member, click "Save and Add Another," enter another member, and so on. This is a major time-saver for clients who are using Drupal to manage a lot of online content.

No, I don't need this, but ooh, it's perty! Modules

The following modules are particularly useful for adding a bit of whiz-bang to your sites.

Views Slideshow (drupal.org/project/views_slideshow (*http://drupal.org/project/views_slideshow*))

Views Slideshow allows you to create customized JQuery slideshows using Views data. This is useful when you want to create a banner of featured content on a site landing page, for example; or if you want to show a list of featured projects on your home page.

Colorbox (drupal.org/project/colorbox (*http://drupal.org/project/colorbox*))

Colorbox is a module that allows you to display images using JQuery overlays.

User Points (drupal.org/project/userpoints (*http://drupal.org/project/userpoints*))

User Points is a helper module that allows you to set up your site to give users "points" for doing things on your site. This is useful for community sites, where you want to encourage users to engage with the site in some way. The User Points project page lists a number of additional modules that the community has created with the help of the User Points module. If you're interested in building a community-oriented site, it's well worth a look.

A completely incomplete listing

As mentioned before, the modules listed above are hardly a complete listing of everything you might need in a Drupal installation. But remember the point: once you know what you need the site to *do*, it's that much easier to find a module that can help you do it. Have fun creating!

CHAPTER 4

Working with Clients

This final chapter deals with walking clients through the Drupal process. It collects what I've learned over years of running a studio and dealing with clients, and also touches on how to collect what you learn over the course of your projects, so that the next one is always just a little bit easier.

Proposing and Estimating Projects

Over the years, I've learned to break the discovery process into two distinct phases. The first, outlined here, happens prior to estimating the project, and gives me the background I need to create a proposal and estimate for the project. The second, more comprehensive phase happens during and after the project kickoff. This phase, described in Chapter 2, is where we start framing the design challenge that we're facing, fleshing out the user experience, and making sure that the client is on board with our approach.

Pre-proposal discovery: what you need to know

The initial discovery phase should give you enough information about the client, the project's goals and the level of complexity that you can put together an accurate proposal. During this phase, you're looking to learn:

- Who is the client?
- How well do they know the business, and themselves?
- Who are they trying to reach?
- What's the real goal here? What are they hoping their site will accomplish for them?
- What kind of functionality are they going to need? Is it something you can handle on your own, or will you need to bring in external resources?

- What's the process for decision making within the organization? Are we dealing one-on-one with the main decision maker, or does everything have to go through one or more layers of red tape before it can be approved?
- What kind of content are we working with? Do they have examples to show? How many pages, sections, etc.? How do they expect people to access or organize the content?
- How big is their budget?
- How open are they to your ideas and approach? What "vibe" do you get from them?

All of these questions should help you get a sense of what it's going to be like to work with the client, and whether you'll be able to create a productive working relationship. During initial conversations with potential clients, I often start putting answers to these questions in a standard Project Brief (available in Appendix A, at the end of this guide), that will get fleshed out in the project kickoff meeting as the beginning of the Discovery phase. I've also included it as a download from my website for potential clients to fill out before we estimate projects. While it doesn't replace an initial phone call, it's very good at helping weed out clients who may be more interested in price-shopping than in hiring a serious design team.

From the Trenches: Richard Banfield, Fresh Tilled Soil

Fresh Tilled Soil, based in Waltham, MA, designs dynamic interfaces for web startups. I sat down with founder and president, Richard Banfield, to discuss how they choose and work with clients.

Dani: You seem to have longer-term relationships, where you are working with clients through multiple iterations of their business. Was that intentional?

Richard: Absolutely. We had an awakening a few years ago, where we realized that we couldn't roll through this roller coaster day by day—where you've got a project and then nothing, and then a project and then nothing. We wanted clients who wanted to work with us as partners, we wanted long-term contracts, we wanted to provide something that couldn't be outsourced to a foreign country—and that means that we had to become high-end consultants providing high-end product development, essentially.

We also decided to spin off the smaller projects to Super Web-O-Matic [a subsidiary business that specializes in affordable Wordpress sites for small business], which takes care of the smaller projects, so we don't get distracted.

If you're a UI/UX Designer, you're essentially a partner to the executive team of the company you're working with. So you can't be anything but the absolute best thought leadership consultant. You're not just a hired gun. If you're a hired gun, certainly you'll be outsourced.

Dani: Even in the UX world, there are people who will think of you as hired guns. They're trying to hire a UX designer because they've heard they need one—and not because they have an investment in the user experience of their product and making something that people actually want to use. Do you find you run into clients like that?

Richard: We established something that we called "the Lens," and it's sort of a way of telling ideal versus non-ideal clients. This lens includes things like: Does this person have the money to do the thing they want to do? Also, is this a challenging and exciting project that we'd feel passionate about? Is this a client that respects the role of a business like ours as a partner to theirs, or are they just going to treat us like a vendor? Is this the type of person that I could sit down and have a beer with? Is there good chemistry there—will we have good communication, or is it always going to be that every single conversation we have has to go through legal counsel, or it's going to be a fight or something?

For entrepreneurial clients, it's something that goes even deeper. For example: Is this a client who's worked on a successful project before? First time entrepreneurs tend to be exhausting, because they think they can do more than they can. They're not really open and coachable. If they haven't gotten a couple of wins or failures under their belt, they're unrealistic about what they can do and can't do.

Dani: I also tend to find that they can be scared about money.

Richard: There's no way that I can do a good job if I'm thinking, "I shouldn't spend that extra hour making this perfect." Mostly, we're non-negotiable on our prices now. It's taken us six years to get to that point where we can say, "This is what we know it's going to cost, because we've done 200 of these projects. No amount of cajoling or arguing is going to change that."

I think that the good clients recognize this immediately—they know what that means, they know what the value is—and they put the checks down. The ones that nickel-and-dime you over every little detail in the contract? Those are red flags. Those are people you don't want to work with.

Pricing a project: Fixed-Bid versus hourly

The question of how to charge for Drupal is a sticky one. On one hand, most significant web projects will carry with them a level of uncertainty that makes an hourly rate attractive. What happens when the client needs extra changes? What happens when a certain functional problem is trickier to solve than you had accounted for, and you end up spending twice as many hours as you had intended? All of these are very valid reasons to charge hourly for your work, and many developers I know have no problem getting clients to agree to hourly billing.

That said, many clients (and designers) prefer a fixed-bid approach. Clients often equate the hourly approach with a ticking clock that must be shut off before things get too expensive, and that often means that quality gets sacrificed in the name of doing things quickly. I've especially seen this in consulting work. For example, working with a client to reposition their brand can require anywhere from 20–100 hours of time to really see results; however, many clients working with an hourly rate will cut the process off as early as 6 hours in, afraid of getting a huge bill at the end of our work together.

As a result, the client doesn't get the results they were hoping for, and they often feel that they wasted their money.

Using a fixed-bid approach attaches a very real and specific value to your work that clients have an easier time dealing with. It also helps with creating consistent income and cash flow; if, during the process of learning Drupal, you find yourself building websites much more quickly than you used to, a fixed bid allows you to charge the same (or higher) than you used to when you were still learning the ropes.

The trick, I have found, to working with fixed bid pricing is the following:

1. *Keep very detailed time records.* Over time, you'll start to realize how long things actually take to build.

2. *Have a contract that specifically states what clients will get from you.* In estimates, I always account for up to three iterations of a site's look and feel, with one opportunity to completely redesign it. Anything above and beyond that becomes a change order, and results in hourly charges.

3. *Work with clients to establish payment schedules.* With smaller clients, I tend to take an initial deposit, and then break the rest of the balance into monthly installments, regardless of when the project is finished. This helps me plan cash flow, while giving the client a chance to budget for the work. Other designers prefer a milestone-based approach, with one installment due upon approval of designs, and another due at the end of the project. Both approaches carry certain risks. With the monthly billing approach, you get paid sooner and more regularly, but it can be harder to define where, exactly, a project ends. With the milestone-based billing approach, you risk running into a negative cash-flow situation at any point where the project runs into delays. And believe me, it will run into delays.

Ultimately, whether you work hourly or fixed bid, you still have to be able to give the client an approximate idea of what their job will cost, and how long it will take to complete. The best process I've seen for estimating Drupal projects comes from CivicActions in San Francisco; their Estimating Spreadsheet* is a brilliant way to break up the individual pieces of a Drupal project by hours needed for specific team members. For working with distributed teams, I find translating the spreadsheet into a Google Doc offers a great way to collaboratively come up with numbers for a proposal.

Writing the proposal

Once you've collected the initial discovery, and estimated what resources you'll need and how much the project will take to build, it's time to craft a proposal. At a minimum, a good proposal should include:

---

* available as an OpenOffice download here: *http://civicactions.com/estimating-worksheet*. It should also open in Mac's Numbers application or Microsoft Excel. I've also imported it as a Google Doc with some success.

- *Your initial assessment of the goals, audience and objectives of the project*, based on your discovery sessions with the client.
- *A statement of work that describes what you'll deliver to the client.* This should include a number of original concepts you'll deliver, as well as how many rounds of revisions included in the budget. It should also include a list of deliverables you'll need from the client in order to proceed, and a note about what happens if they're late on their deliverables.
- *Estimated prices for the project you're discussing.* Many teams like to give a low and a high bid, with the note that pricing is based on the information you have on hand, and that new information, such as additional stakeholders or new content that wasn't discussed up front, may push the project into the upper price range.
- *Any terms and conditions that apply to the project.* This should include things like a schedule, what happens if you or the client decide to cancel the project, and how you'll deal with issues such as delays or new information.

In addition to these things, some teams find it helpful to include:

- *An overview of the design and development process*, which gives the client an idea of what to expect.
- *Case studies or images of previous design work* done for other clients.
- *A more detailed scope of work*, which would include Drupal-level deliverables, such as custom page templates or content types included in the estimated cost. Include this information with caution; not all clients understand "DrupalSpeak™," and it could cause confusion.
- *Bios of team members*, and other information about the company.

In my own work with clients, I use two proposal formats. For larger projects, especially ones where I have to put together a team for the project, I use a proposal format adapted from Chicago design firm Rogue Element's proposals[†]. The format has the benefit of being both concise and comprehensive, and it's easily adaptable to any studio's needs.

For shorter projects, I use an amended proposal, or Work Agreement, that includes just the first set of information above. I use this format for smaller projects (for example, budgets around $5k or less), or for repeat clients. For new clients, I may also include a bit of information about the studio and a list of previous design work.

A sample of both the proposal and Work Agreement is available in Appendix A. The content is unique to my studio and the client involved, but the format is free for you to adapt as you need to.

[†] Which you can find in this article: *http://www.howdesign.com/article/proposal/*

Getting clients to love you, even when you have to tell them "no" (and what to do if they don't)

There comes a time in every Drupal project where you are going to have to say "no" to something your client wants. This could happen for a number of reasons. Your client could have seen an amazing widget on somebody else's site and feels that they MUST have it on theirs. Or they decide all of a sudden that what they really need to "engage their community" is a full set of social media tools that customers can use directly through their site. No matter what the reason is, you've already set the scope for the project, you're probably already worried about meeting the deadlines you have, and you need to find a way to diffuse this situation without losing your patience or the client.

There are a few things to remember when this happens to you.

- Most of the time, the client will actually have a very good reason for making this suggestion.
- Just because something can't be part of the site now doesn't mean it can't ever be; in fact, often these types of conversations lead to future enhancements down the line.
- What the client needs from you is to know that they've been heard, and to know what you're going to do about it.

This is why it's so essential to have up-front documentation that clearly describes the technical and design scope of the project, user objectives and business goals. The documentation won't prevent these ideas from cropping up; what it will do is give you a foundation for the conversation you need to have with the client when they do.

For example, let's say that you contracted with the client to build a simple, mostly promotional site with an events listing, news page, blog and contact form. You've gotten through the discovery phase and have already started theming and approving designs, when the client realizes that she'd really love to add some interaction to the mix. She's seen other companies that have forums where users hang out, converse and help each other. She's heard that Drupal "makes it easy" to add forums to a website, and she wants to implement it straightaway.

First, does Drupal actually "make it easy" to add a forum to your site? Technically, yes. Forums are part of Drupal's core functionality, and you can enable the forum simply by clicking a button on the Modules page. However, enabling the forum is just a tiny piece of what's actually involved in creating a forum. You have to figure out where it belongs in the site's architecture, decide who has access and who doesn't, set up the appropriate permissions, and style it to mesh with the look and feel of the rest of the site. Also, the client will have to promote the forums, create categories for forum topics, get people actually using them, and monitor them consistently for trolls and spammers. What we think of as "easy" at first glance rarely is once we're in the process of making it happen.

There are several ways to approach the challenge of pushing back, most of which will at some point involve referring the client back to the documentation you created at the beginning of your project. My personal approach is to say, "Great idea! Let me ask just a few questions to figure out how this can work..." This assures the client that you're listening to them, but also helps them talk through the business logic behind the request, and understand all that actually goes into making their request happen. Often, this approach will either talk them out of the idea completely or put it in the works for the next iteration of the site. Either response is a good resolution.

To elaborate on this example, any of the following questions could work with most reasonable clients, depending on where you are in the project plan:

> "A forum could be great! How were you planning on promoting it? Do you have resources to monitor it for spammers and trolls?"

> "I like that idea, but one of our business objectives was to focus on the organization's human-friendly approach to customer service. A user forum might give the impression that you prefer your customers to handle issues among themselves. What do you expect the user will gain from the forum?"

> "That sounds like a great idea, but right now, our push is to get the basic functionality into the site before launch on Tuesday. Do you want to have a discussion about adding it to the next iteration of the site? I'll work up some estimates on what it would cost."

There are a few things to note about this approach. First, clients really love it when you tell them they've had a great idea. Second, you're making it clear that although the idea is good, they have to be prepared to do some work to make it happen.

Third, and this is the really important part: *you're not pointing to a specific document and saying "if you remember the piece of paper you signed..."*

In my early days of working with clients, I used the "that's not in the contract" line frequently, and it never ever worked. Something about referring people back to legal agreements sets up the conversation to be combative; the client ends up perceiving that you're trying to pick a fight with them. Referring to themes that you'd agreed on in the course of discovery shows the client that you're interested to see how this new idea might work with what has already agreed upon, and you want to find a solution that works for everybody.

This process of dealing with client requests that push a project beyond the original scope has caused some teams to adopt a hybrid Agile approach to Drupal projects. While the process still involves defining the scope of work and planning things out up front, design and development happen together, iteratively and collaboratively. This helps teams keep everyone on track while accounting for the inevitable bumps in the road that come with designing for Drupal. Says Four Kitchens' Todd Nienkerk of their Agile process:

> We rarely say "no" to a client with regard to functionality, but we do explain that:
>
> 1. Adding something before launch means something else needs to be pushed back;

2. Their current budget doesn't really allow for this extra work, so let's reprioritize or find more money, etc.

Scrum provides a very handy framework for this discussion because all ideas, regardless of how enormous or superfluous or whim-driven they may be, go into the project backlog for future discussion. Usually having it in the backlog—i.e., captured somewhere for the client to see every so often—is enough to make them happy and never actually push for that feature to be implemented.

That's easy for you to say...

Of course, this approach doesn't always work. Occasionally, you run into the type of client that I like to call "the Dictator." They grab ideas completely out of left field and present you with them, and you're expected to take that idea and run with it. If you try to spin the conversation back to the scope that was agreed upon, they get hostile and say things like "this is what I hired you to do," or "just make it happen."

Or, worse, you run into the type of client that loves everything you do, gives you complete creative freedom, and gives you absolutely no direction, feedback, or restraints—but will come up with an idea once a week that absolutely won't fit into the budget, and she can't understand why when you explain it to her.

When you run into these types of clients, you have to make a choice. Is it more important to preserve the client relationship, or to stand your ground and risk walking away from the project?

I'm fortunate in my career to have grown skilled at managing "difficult" clients. But the most important part of this skill is knowing myself well enough to know the types of clients that I just can't work with. In my entire career, the handful of times that a project has gone sour can be directly attributed to deciding to take on a project despite the obvious conflicts between myself and the client. If you're on a team, it can be easier; you have other team members who you can lean on when things get to be more than you can handle. If you're working solo, or as part of a small distributed team, it can make you wonder why you got into this field in the first place.

Either way, part of managing your career is learning how to navigate difficult situations with grace. If you find yourself faced with a client who refuses to hear the word "no," it's on you to evaluate whether their request can be accommodated within the current budget, and to make any adjustments that need to be made, including possibly letting the client go.

The "Professional Relationship" clause

Recently, I gave a brief talk on the state of designers and UXers in the typical Drupal team. During discussions after the talk, I mentioned the "Professional Relationship" clause that I include in all of my Work Agreements, that establishes the working relationship I expect with clients, and states that I (or the client) can terminate the agreement if one of us isn't living up to the terms of this relationship. This statement—that

I basically told clients how I expected them to treat me, and what they could expect of me in return—was met with expressions of shock and curiosity by everyone in the room, most of whom were developers.

The reason I put the clause into my contracts was simple; as a self-employed designer, I'm selling my time and energy. If that time and energy is being sapped by abusive or disrespectful clients, I need to be able to address the situation proactively in a way that protects my business and my sanity. The "Professional Relationship" clause, which encompasses a few bullet points on the front page of the contract, helps clients understand that I'm here to help them—and if they won't respect that, they should find someone else to work with.

I put the clause into my contracts with the help of Jessica Manganello, a client, friend, and co-founder of New Leaf Legal‡, a terrific team of entrepreneurial lawyers in the Boston area. She and I got together to look at my contracts after a particularly nasty situation with a client who turned abusive after ignoring his project for over a year. Although he had clearly breached his end of the contract, I had also set up my initial contract, which was cobbled together from sample contracts I got from a copy of *Legal Forms for Graphic Designers* (Allworth Press) and the AIGA's website§, with no way for me to get out of a project that wasn't working out. Establishing the clause helped me make it extra clear to clients that I meant business, and I've yet to meet the client who refused to sign as a result of the clause.

If you want to consider adding the clause to your contracts, you can find it in my sample Work Agreement in Appendix A. If you want a contract that fully covers all your bases and makes sure that you're covered for anything, give Jess at New Leaf a call.

After the Handoff: The project retrospective

"Unfortunately, this critical step [of reflecting on a project after its completion] is nearly always ignored by professional designers. Assessment implies internal criticism, something many companies prefer to leave up to public relations or external product reviews. The assessment [of the project's success] must be at a user and project level, rather than a quality assurance level, and benchmarks for success have generally not been developed or acknowledged within corporate America. In many high-pressure design consultancies, to reflect is to waste time. Reflection is not productive and is frequently viewed as a poor use of money and resources."‖

The case study. Some designers swear by them as a valuable marketing tool; others refuse to do them, insisting that there's just "too much work to do," or insisting that images of their work will speak for themselves. I've even heard designers say that clients

---

‡ *http://newleaflegal.com*

§ The AIGA (American Institute of Graphic Arts) is the international association of graphic designers, based in the US. *http://aiga.org*

‖ Kolko, Jonathan. *Thoughts on Interaction Design*, p. 34

don't like reading case studies. I've never personally seen this, but then, I've never quite subscribed to the idea of being "too busy to read."

Let me state one thing emphatically: *reflecting on your work—whether you share them as case studies or not—is vitally important to your career as a designer.* Whether you're part of a team, an independent designer, or working in corporate America, the time that you take to think over a project—how it went, what went right, how you can make things better next time—is one of the most important things that can you can do. Every time I've taken the time to reflect on a project, no matter how well or how horribly it went, I've learned something valuable that I can take into the future. Reflecting on "nightmare" projects has proven particularly valuable; not only does it give me a way to move on from them productively, it also gives me a wellspring of lessons for those inevitable "have you ever had a project that just went *horribly?*" questions that clients or job interviewers sometimes like to spring on you.

The time that you take to reflect at the end of a project depends on the project, and often on your role in the project. When I'm leading a project I've done before and all goes well, a simple retrospective can take as little as a half hour with a coffee and my journal; if I'm part of a larger team, or if the project hits some bumps in the road I wasn't anticipating, it can take much longer. The process you use is up to you, but the goals are often the same:

1. Identify what was involved in the project that made it unique;
2. Identify any factors that worked particularly well. This could be the client, your style of communication, a new kind of documentation—anything that contributed to this project going well.
3. Identify any factors that made the project harder than it needed to be. This is an area I tend to spend the most time on. When I reflect on a project, I want to know what I can improve on the next time, see if there were any areas I need to develop more skill in.
4. Document the things that will be particularly useful for later projects. This may be code, or it may be a way of dealing with clients; whatever it is, make sure you have it set aside somewhere where you can find it again.

The key to doing a successful retrospective is to find a process that works for you. Sometimes, long-form prose works, like a blog entry or journalling. Sometimes, if I'm stuck, I'll use a Mind Map to get all of my thoughts out on a page before I commit anything to prose. (For more on Mind Maps, check out Chapter 2.)

Including clients in the retrospective

The choice of whether to include clients in your post-project reflections is completely up to you. Asking clients for feedback, especially if the project didn't go as well as you'd hoped, can be hard. Nobody likes to hear that they were harsher than they needed to be in a particular conversation, or that their design solutions weren't particularly good.

Whether you choose to allow clients into the retrospective process or not, getting feedback from clients is an essential part of the growth process, and it can also provide useful information for future projects. Designer Todd Nienkerk of Four Kitchens says:

> "We frame the conversation by saying that we won't take anything personally and by leading off with some thoughtful self-criticism to get the conversation started. As you say, it can sting, but it's important to learn what needs attention and growth."

There are several ways to include client feedback in your post-project reflection. The easiest way is through simple surveys; whether you do them through an online service like Survey Monkey or through a simple thank-you note with a questionnaire, asking the right questions can get some very valuable feedback. While surveys can be valuable, I often find that a simple conversation, over the phone or over coffee, works best. For one, it's more likely that the client will actually give you feedback (often a challenge with other means of communication); second; it gives you a valuable chance both to deepen your relationship with the client and find out if there's additional projects in the pipeline that you can create a pitch for.

Documenting what you learned

An important benefit of the project Retrospective is being able to document what you've learned. This could be a new way of collaborating with clients, a new productivity tool, or a new module that you can't wait to share your glee about. How you set up this documentation is, again, up to you, but the best documentation is:

- **Searchable** (so you can find notes when you need them);
- **Sharable** (so when you're chatting with another Drupal buddy who's dealing with a problem you've had before, you can send them a link to it);
- **Has the option of being private**. Let's face it: if a project really sucked, the last thing you want to do is blog about it publicly. But there's knowledge to be gained from it, regardless, and you want to be able to document what you've learned so you can remember it next time.

Every team has their own way of collecting documentation. Some will make their own wikis in Drupal, or use OpenAtrium#, a Drupal-based project intranet created by DC-based Drupal shop Development Seed. Others will collect documentation in a personal blog, built in Drupal or Wordpress.

Evernote* is a free cross-platform application that allows you to easily collect, tag and share notes by e-mail, and it syncs your notes over the Internet without forcing you to be online in order to create or edit your notes (Figure 4-1). You can also organize your content into distinct notebooks, which is incredibly useful when you want to separate, for example, theming notes from modules you want to check out. And, it's available

---

\#openatrium.com (*http://openatrium.com*)

* evernote.com (*http://evernote.com*)

for iPad, iPhone and Android, so collecting notes is super-easy if you don't always have your computer on you.

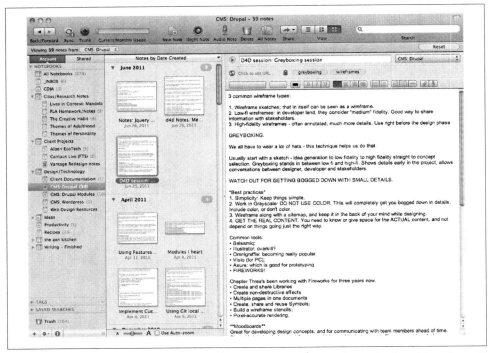

Figure 4-1. Evernote lets you collect and organize notes in topic-specific notebooks. I like to keep all of my Drupal notes in two notebooks: one for more general Drupal knowledge, and another for specific modules.

Another thing that's very handy to collect is code snippets. These can also be saved in Evernote, published as blog posts, or—if you're using Coda†, my favorite Mac OSX-based site editor, you can save snippets directly in the program's Clips library (Figure 4-2), and double-click on them to add them to your file as you're coding. This is especially useful for common Drupal theme hooks, or for commonly used CSS, Javascript or HTML snippets.

† panic.com/coda (*http://panic.com/coda*)

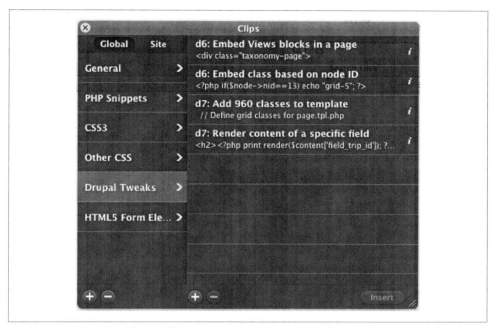

Figure 4-2. Coda's Clips library allows you to save and organize code snippets that you can easily add to your site's theme files. This is extremely useful once you start learning how to mess with theme hooks and .tpl files.

Documenting for the community

Dries Buytaert, creator of Drupal, has been quoted many times as saying that the Drupal community needs designers. But what the community also needs is more people to help document Drupal modules, best practices, and other things that can help Drupal newbies not cry their way through their first several Drupal projects. While many development teams have made a habit of blogging their Drupal knowledge, too many contributed modules on Drupal.org have woefully inadequate documentation, which makes it harder for folks new to Drupal who aren't hardcore programmers to access the brilliance of these modules. If, at the end of a project, you find yourself with knowledge of a particular module that isn't being shared, consider contributing documentation on Drupal.org (*http://drupal.org*), or on your own blog. The community will love you for it.

Project Brief

NOTE: This brief borrows heavily from Happy Cog's project planner (*http://www.hap pycog.com/*), with a bent towards both branding and Drupal projects. I made this available as a download from the the zen kitchen's website; clients would download it in Word, fill it out and send it back to us before we got back to them with a proposal. This can be very handy for getting a head-start on the discovery process.

Hey there! It's nice to meet you.

This handy worksheet is designed to help us get a feel for your organization's background, goals and design needs, and to help make sure that everyone is on the same page so that we can create the most accurate proposal possible for your project. The information in this document is also an important part of the zen kitchen's proven design process—your answers here serve an important role in clarifying direction, messaging and audience up front. This makes it easier for us to produce award-winning strategic design for our clients.

When you're finished, save the document as *{organization name}_*`planner.doc` (replacing *{organization name}* with the name of your particular organization), and email the document to *email@site.com*. Please allow up to 1 week for a response. In a hurry? Just let us know and we'll let you know if we can help you sooner.

While this project planner includes information that will help us for identity, print and web projects, it also includes some information that is specific to certain types of projects. Feel free to leave out any information that doesn't apply to your project; however, the background information, look and feel, and other supporting information is something that we need for all types of projects.

Who are you?

Your name:
First and Last Name

Your title:
Answer here.

Organization name:
Answer here.

Where is your office located? (not necessarily where your organization is, where you are):
Answer here.

Email address and URL (if you have one):
Enter email address here

Enter URL here

Business phone including area and/or country code:
Phone number here

So, how did you hear about us?
Answer here.

Responding to inquiries generally takes up to a week. If you need us to move more quickly than that, please indicate below:
[ ] I'm in a rush and I need a Proposal/Statement of Work from you as soon as possible

About your project

Tell us about your project. What components will be involved? *Check (√) all that apply.*

{ } Logo/Identity Design
{ } Business cards, stationery, etc.
{ } Brochure, postcards, sales or tradeshow materials
{ } Design for events
{ } Annual or Corporate Citizenship/Responsibility/Sustainability Report
{ } Website Design
{ } E-mail marketing
{ } Print advertising

Have you ever worked with a designer or design firm before? What was that experience like? What type of project? What worked? What didn't?
Answer here.

Background

Tell us in a few words about your organization. What do you produce? Why does your customer need it?
Answer here.

How many people does your organization employ? Who besides you (if applicable) will be decision-makers on this project?
Answer here.

Goals and Objectives

What is your organization looking to achieve with strategic design? *(i.e., increased visibility? More sales? Build customer loyalty? General image upgrade? Other?) Please be specific and try to stick with one major goal with 1–2 secondary goals.*
Answer here.

How will you define success for this project?
Answer here.

Target Audience

List some key facts about your intended market or user. Include both demographic data *(age, income, education, etc.)* ***and psychographics*** *(what magazines do they read? What websites do they visit frequently? What are their values and attitudes?).*
Answer here.

Does your target audience already know about your product or service? If so, how do they feel about it? How would you like to change that perception *(if at all)?*
Answer here.

What motivates them to use your product or service?
Answer here.

For websites: Who do you consider the primary and secondary users of your site? What are they there for? What information do you want to give them?
Answer here.

Competition

Who do you consider your peers and competitors? How do they present themselves? *Give us their URLs if you have them.*
Answer here.

What are the key benefits/advantages to going with you instead of your competitors?
Answer here.

How about your competitors? Do consumers perceive any advantages to going with them? (It's okay to be honest here. Part of good design is knowing what your competitors do well so we can differentiate from them.)
> Answer here.

Brand attributes

Describe briefly, in as few words as possible, the type of feelings that you want to evoke in the audience with your brand and/or web presence, and the brand attributes that you want to convey. (Example feelings may include: warmth, reassurance, excitement, empowerment. Example brand attributes: integrity, honesty, trustworthiness.)
> Answer here.

Using adjectives and short phrases, tell us about the look and feel you're going for. (Examples: edgy, modern, clean, organic, traditional, classic, user-friendly. Try to avoid terms like "web 2.0" and "cutting edge.")
> Answer here.

In terms of look and feel, are there any sites or design projects you've seen that you feel convey the type of image you're going for? Share a few of them and tell us why they appeal to you.
> Answer here.

Functionality and Technical Requirements

For all projects:

Are there any current brand standards that we should be aware of adhering to: Fonts, colors, etc.? If not, would you like to talk about having us develop them for you?
> Answer here.

How much of the copy do you have completed for this project?

> { } All of it
> { } Some of it
> { } We'd like to hire you to create it

For print projects:

How will you be handling distribution of design? (Are brochures mailed or handed out? Will ads run on a specific schedule?)
> Answer here.

Do you have a printer currently, or do you want us to handle it for you? *(Note: design estimates do not include printing costs, which will be handled separately by the client. Also, as a sustainable design firm, the zen kitchen promotes and works exclusively with companies that utilize sustainably-minded printing methods.)*
Answer here.

For web projects:

Is your current site powered by a content management system (CMS) or publishing platform? How are updates generally handled?
Answer here.

If "yes," which platform are you using?
Answer here.

What do you like/dislike about it?
Answer here.

Does your site plan involve support for community features, social media, RSS feeds, profiles, commenting, blogs, forums, sharing, user-generated content, etc? *Give us a brief rundown of what you'd like to see.*
Answer here.

Does your plan include hosting video, audio or other media-intensive components? *This could involve podcasting, photo sharing, etc.*
Answer here.

Does your plan include selling products, event management, or other features that would require a user to give you money through the site?
Answer here.

About how many pages do you estimate your site will have? What might the top-level navigation look like *(main sections, secondary sections, etc.)?*
Answer here.

Would you prefer to do this project in a single pass or split it up into phases *(each requiring its own budget)?*
Answer here.

If splitting up into phases, please tell us the general breakdown of each phase that you have in mind.
Answer here.

Anything else we should know?
Answer here.

To deliver the best experience to the most users and to build pages that will last, we use modern standards-based methods. As a result, our sites may not look exactly the same in an old, non-compliant browser like Internet Explorer 6 as they do in newer browsers like Firefox, Safari, and Internet Explorer 7 and 8. Designing your site to work in older, non-compliant browsers will add significant development time and cost to the project budget, and some modern technologies that aren't supported by the browser may have to be removed from the project scope.

{ } My site has to look and work exactly the same way in older as it does in newer browsers.
{ } I understand that the site may not look as good or work as well in an outdated browsers.

Time and money

If you're working within a time frame, or have been given a mandatory launch date, list it here. If the project will launch in phases, list proposed milestones and dates.
Answer here.

Please tell us your budget for this project. (Note: Sharing a realistic assessment of what you have to spend on this effort will help us scope our engagement appropriately. While disclosing your budget might not be something you typically do, sharing this information with us now will greatly reduce the likelihood of both sides spending significant time and resources "shooting in the dark.")
Answer here.

Thanks again!

We very much appreciate you taking the time to fill out our project planner. We realize it's a lot to ask up front, but it's a huge help when it comes time to put together numbers that accurately reflect the work involved in your unique.

When you're finished, save the document as *{organization name}*_planner.doc (replacing *{organization name}* with the name of your particular organization), and email the document to *email@site.com*. Please allow up to 1 week for a response. In a hurry? Just let us know and we'll let you know if we can help you sooner.

THIS INFORMATION IS USED TO DEVELOP AND IMPLEMENT PROCEDURES IN CREATING THE PROJECT REQUESTED. BY SIGNING THIS AGREEMENT, YOU AGREE ALL INFORMATION SUBMITTED IS CORRECT.

Name (print)
Approval Signature
Date
Designer Approval

Work Agreement (with Professional Relationship Clause)

NOTE: The terms of this standard Work Agreement were crafted by Jessica Manganello, founding attorney at New Leaf Legal (*http://newleaflegal.com*). They're available for you to adapt under the Creative Commons license; however, if you need a great legal team to help you work out your own contract terms, I highly suggest giving the team at New Leaf a call sometime.

Work Agreement

Description	Amount
Brand and Messaging Strategy, including:	*$XXX*
One half-day kickoff meeting to brainstorm audience profiles, needs and perceptions, key messages and platforms	
Brand immersion and research	
Compilation of research findings and recommendations into a comprehensive findings analysis and preliminary messaging report	
Refinement of findings and positioning into comprehensive brand position and key messaging report.	
Project Management and client communication (including up to 2 followup meetings)	
Design of Drupal website, including:	*$XXX*
Wireframes, user flows and site maps to flesh out user experience priorities	
Creation of site look and feel, including 3 rounds of revisions and 1 complete change of direction (if needed)	
Project Management and client communication	
Configuration of Drupal website, including:	*$XXX*
Installation and configuration of Drupal CMS;	
Establishment of user roles and permissions, including content editors and administrators;	

Description	Amount
Project Management and client communication	
Theming of Drupal website, including:	$XXX
Application of site look and feel across all site page templates.	
Creation of up to 5 unique page templates	
Estimate Total	**$XXXXX**

Terms and Conditions

This work agreement is based on the specifications listed in the above Project Scope. If, upon receipt of all materials to be supplied by client, the project is determined to differ significantly from the original specifications, the client will be notified promptly and an updated estimate will be produced. This estimate does not include expenses and reimbursements aside from those listed in the Estimated Costs and Project Scope. If such expenses arise, the client will be informed prior to expenditures made and a separate invoice will be submitted for reimbursement.

Payment Notes

Payment will be made in 5 installments monthly starting upon project signoff. The first installment of $XXXX is due before project starts; 4 installments of $XXXX each will be due on the fifth of each month starting in March 2011.

All estimates are valid for 30 days from the date of estimate.

Payment Notes:

A finance charge of 5% per month will be applied to overdue balances. A charge of $25 per item will be charged for checks returned by the bank.

Professional Relationship

In order to provide a rewarding working experience for both Client and Designer, Designer seeks to maintain a professional relationship with the Client. Designer and Client agree to:

- Promptly meet deadlines for producing material, payments, and/or work product and communicate clearly if those deadlines can not be met with alternative timelines for delivery.

- Promptly review and reply to communications from parties involved in this project

Deliverables Timeframe

- Milestones and dates/times will be determined in initial project meeting once contract is approved and deposit is received. Once project starts, a detailed action plan will be submitted to client and we will establish deadlines for delivery on content one piece at a time.

- Failure of client to provide the required materials within the established deadlines will result in a delay of all deliverable deadlines. This delay will be equal to the number of days late the materials were received by the Designer, unless otherwise specified in writing, via e-mail, by Designer.

Additional Terms

Rejection/Cancellation of Project

The client shall not unreasonably withhold acceptance of, or payment for, the project. If, prior to completion of the project, the client observes any nonconformance with the design plan, the Designer must be promptly notified, allowing for necessary corrections. Cancellation or Rejection by Client must be made upon 10 days written notice to Designer. Rejection of the completed project or cancellation during its execution will result in forfeiture of the deposit and billing for all additional labor or expenses incurred prior to the date of cancellation, at the standard rate of $*XXX* per hour.

All elements created by the Designer for the project must then be returned to the Designer within 30 days of cancellation. All materials supplied by the Client will be returned in their original condition within 30 days of cancellation. Any usage by the Client of design elements created by the Designer after cancellation of the project will result in appropriate legal action. Client shall bear all costs, expenses, and reasonable attorney's fees in any action brought to recover payment, enforce the terms and or protect Designer's Intellectual Property under this contract.

Designer reserves the right to cancel this contract at any time upon 10 days written notice for any reason, including but not limited to: clients failure to provide materials or payment within 30 days of the agreed upon deadlines or failure of client to comply with the terms of this agreement including the terms of the Professional Relationship clause. Upon Designer's cancellation of the contract, Designer will return all unused funds and deposits to the Client and return all materials to the Client within 30 days of cancellation.

Modifications

Modification of the Agreement must be written, except that the invoice may include, and the Client shall pay, any fees or expenses that were orally authorized by the Client in order to progress promptly with the work. Oral agreements and other communications will be confirmed in writing, including electronically, and thereby incorporated into this agreement.

Ownership of Artwork

The Designer retains ownership of all original artwork, whether preliminary or final. No use of same shall be made, nor any ideas obtained therefrom used, except upon compensation to be determined by the Designer. The client shall return such artwork within thirty (30) days of use. In the case of logo work, the client shall retain ownership of artwork once the invoice has been paid in full and can use said logo in all of their materials, including materials created by other designers. Said artwork, however, may not be modified for any use without the express consent of the Designer.

The Designer retains the right to use the completed project and any preliminary designs for the purpose of design competitions, future publications on design, educational purposes, and marketing materials. Where applicable the client will be given any necessary credit for usage of the project elements.

Reproduction of Work

The client assumes full reproduction rights upon payment for completed project. The work may be reproduced as is by the client at any given time. Any revisions to the work prior to reproduction must be negotiated between the Designer and the client.

Author's Alterations (AA's)

AA's represent work performed in addition to the original concept and specifications. Such work includes, but is not limited to: inclusion of material in project in addition to material originally discussed; additional design concepts or revisions of project beyond the number allotted in the project scope section of this contract; significant color/paper/quantity changes beyond what was originally discussed.

Such additional work shall be charged at a rate of $*XXX* per hour plus any additional expenses incurred by the extra work (including rush shipping and/or printing charges), and will be supported with documentation upon request.

No additional payment shall be made for minor changes required to conform to the original assignment description as noted in the creative brief, including spelling and grammatical errors.

The terms of this paragraph do not apply to the agreed upon alterations, modifications, or edits listed in the Deliverables TimeFrame.

The Designer shall not be held responsible for delays in production caused by Author's Alterations.

Proofs

Proofs will be sent to Client via e-mailed PDF unless otherwise noted in the Project Scope section of this contract. Client will be responsible for carefully reviewing said proofs and offering feedback in a timely and constructive manner. Delays in receipt of appropriate feedback by Client will result in delay of project deliverables. A reasonable variation in color between color proofs and the completed job shall constitute acceptable delivery. The Designer cannot be held responsible for errors under any or all of the following conditions: if the Client has failed to return proofs with indication of changes; if the Client has failed to approve proofs in writing via e-mail or signed Approval Form; if the Client has instructed the Designer to proceed without submission of proofs.

Completion/Delivery of Project

The estimated completion date of the project is to be determined. Any shipping or insurance costs will be assumed by the client. Any alteration or deviation from the above specifications involving extra costs will be executed only upon approval with the client. Any delay in the completion of the project due to failure of client to meet the deadlines set forth in this contract for receipt of materials to begin work on the project, proof revisions/approvals, etc. will delay the completion/delivery date. The Client will allow a reasonable time for printing and shipping of final project (generally 2–3 weeks). The Client will be responsible for any "rush charges" assessed by the printer and/or shipping company due to failure of client to meet the deadlines set forth in this contract for receipt of materials, proof revisions/approvals, etc.

In addition, unusual transportation delays, unforeseen illness, or external forces beyond the control of the Designer, shall entitle the Designer to extend the completion/delivery date, upon notifying the client, by the time equivalent to the period of such delay.

Releases

The Client shall indemnify the Designer against all claims and expenses, including reasonable attorneys' fees, due to uses of design or art work, for which no release was requested in writing or for uses that exceed authority granted by a release. The Client further indemnifies the Designer against any liability, clients, or rights of any third party arising out of this contract, including reasonable attorney's fees and expenses. Client is liable for any costs, including attorney's fees, incurred by Designer in enforcing this agreement and any of its terms.

Any revisions to the work prior to reproduction must be negotiated between the Designer and the client.

Limitation of Liability

The Client agrees that it shall not hold the Designer or his/her agents or employees liable for any incidental or consequential damages which may arise from the Designer's failure to perform any aspect of the Project in a timely manner, regardless of whether such failure was caused by intentional or negligent acts or omissions of the Designer or a third party.

Warranty of Originality

The Designer warrants and represents that, to the best of his/her knowledge, the work assigned hereunder is original and has not been previously published, that consent to use has been obtained on an unlimited basis; the undersigned from third parties is original or, if previously published, that consent to use has been obtained on an un-limited basis; that the Designer has full authority to make this agreement; and that the work prepared by the Designer does not contain any scandalous, libelous, or unlawful matter.

This warranty does not extend to any uses that the Client or others may make of the Designer's product that may infringe on the rights of others. Client expressly agrees that it will hold the Designer harmless for all liability caused by the Client's use of the Designer's product to the extent that such use may infringe on the rights of others.

Project Proposal

NOTE: The format of this proposal was inspired by Chicago design firm Rogue Element, whose founder Alison Manley is a colleague and friend. It's been adapted several times to fit individual project plans, but the basic format is the same.

Project Proposal

> to: Client Name
> Client Address
> Client Phone Number
> for: Project Name
> 1.0 Project Background & Objectives
> 2.0 Statement of Work
> 3.0 Development Process
> 4.0 Budget Estimate
> 5.0 Background & Capabilities
> 6.0 Terms and Conditions

Section 1.0: Project Background and Objectives

The Consulting Firm is the next evolution of a former partnership as a solo endeavor. In this evolution, The Consulting Firm's founder is getting back to what she does well —providing education, consulting and guidance to technology companies in staying compliant with evolving environmental policy. For this, she needs:

- A comprehensive brand platform and core messaging strategy that will guide the brand's communication efforts;

- A social media and blogging strategy that will position The Founder more effectively as a thought leader in the field of environmental compliance for technology, without taking up her entire schedule.

- A website and identity that will help facilitate The Founder's thought leadership efforts, and lead her audience to the brand.

Objective 1: Build upon the history of the Founder's experience with her prior firms to effectively position The Consulting Firm as a leader in environmental compliance information and consulting for technology products.

Effective positioning requires a deep understanding both your brand's target prospects, and an understanding of the landscape that the prospect is dealing with. We will work with The Founder to get a clear picture of the competitive landscape, and establish the right positioning for the brand.

Objective 2: Create a blogging and social media engagement strategy that allows The Founder to more firmly establish thought leadership in the field.

We will work with The Founder to create a content strategy that will allow her to showcase her considerable knowledge in this space, without "giving the cow away" for free. We'll also work with her to set up strategies and tools to manage her online presence without requiring a full time investment.

Objective 3: Create a website that will serve as a marketing vehicle for The Consulting Firm, and integrate The Founder's content leadership efforts.

Using the flexibility of the Drupal content management system, we will create a dynamic website that will allow The Founder to keep content fresh and updated as the business evolves.

Section 2.0: Statement of Work

Brand Messaging and Positioning Strategy

- All deliverables as outlined in the Project Development Process (section 3.0);
- up to 12 hours of collaboration via Skype and in-person meetings to clarify and confirm goals, messaging and brand direction;
- Research and development of brand platform (proposed positioning statement, audience and competitive analysis), and core messaging, using the process outlined in the Project Development Process;

Blogging, Social Media and Content Strategy

- All deliverables as outlined in the Project Development Process (section 3.0);
- up to 12 hours of collaboration via Skype and in-person meetings to clarify and confirm goals, messaging and direction;
- Research and development of social media strategy (blog platform, areas of focus, content guidelines);
- Assistance with setting up profiles and third-party integrations;

Logo and website development

- Setup and delivery of logo, brand guidelines and Drupal website.

Client Responsibilities

To move the project forward efficiently, you will be expected to provide the following:

- Timely delivery of focused feedback, content and edits according to the production schedule;
- Access to preliminary research and competitor materials;
- Participation in face-to-face meetings at key milestones during the project, including the project kickoff meeting and brainstorming sessions.

Section 3.0: Development Process

At the zen kitchen, we believe that the best design results from active and open collaboration between creatives and clients. Our proven, research-driven process helps us consistently create effective, award-winning design that works hard for your business.

Phase I: Strategy, Goal-setting, Requirements & Research

All of our projects begin by working with you to drill down to the core of your messaging, audience and goals. During this first phase, we will refine our understanding of your business, your target audience, and the competition. It is also our objective to clearly identify the project's goals, and define what success will look like. Finally, we will further define the functional, technical, and information requirements for your project which will enable to design the right solution for your needs before getting into the actual Web development. The deliverables for this stage will include:

- A finalized design brief describing our understanding of the project's goals, functional requirements and audience;
- A detailed schedule to guide the process, provided through our project management system.

Phase II: Creative Exploration & Design Development

Through creative thinking, collaborative discourse and a healthy dose of intuition, we develop ideas to visually ex- press your core message. Every choice, from layout and color to type size and style, is made with your communication goals in mind. The best ideas are further refined into initial concepts, which we will present to you. From there, we discuss and refine to turn these concepts into comprehensive design directions. The deliverables for this stage will include:

- Three to four strategic design concepts for evaluation;
- Refinement of your chosen design direction.

Phase III: Implementation and Testing

Once the design direction is approved it's time to implement. At this phase we push pixels, lay out pages, configure, code and collaborate to make sure that each element we produce aligns with your communication goals. During this phase, we also work with you to create and/or gather needed text and images, and incorporate them into the production flow.

We proof and refine the design, test, de-bug, proof again, and prepare for final production or launch. For all of our websites, we perform cross-browser checking on IE7 (and above), Firefox for PC and Mac, and Safari to ensure that the design works perfectly cross-browser. We work closely with all vendors—print, web or otherwise—to ensure that your finished product meets our (and your) standards of excellence.

The deliverables for this stage will include:

- Production management and delivery of the finished project.
- Documentation and training as needed for brand guidelines, updating web content, etc.

Phase VI: Measure and Refine

Our work isn't done after the project delivers. We want to know how it's working. We work with you to gather feed- back, and evaluate not only how the process went, but also what the response has been from the target audiences. At this point, we'll also work together to identify areas of the project that can be refined for future iterations, and develop a plan for the next phase of production.

Section 4.0: Budget Estimate

The following is a proposed budget based on the scope of the project as outlined in this proposal. All fees are our best estimates based on our conversations about the project, and may change as the project moves forward.

the zen kitchen will regularly provide detailed invoices and status updates re: project budget, milestones, etc. via our project management system.

Description of Work	Estimated Fees
Brand and Messaging Strategy, including:	$XXX
One half-day kickoff meeting to brainstorm audience profiles, needs and perceptions, key messages and platforms	
Brand immersion and research	
Compilation of research findings and recommendations into a comprehensive findings analysis and preliminary messaging report	
Refinement of findings and positioning into comprehensive brand position and key messaging report.	
Project Management and client communication (including up to 2 followup meetings)	
Design of Drupal website, including:	$XXX
Wireframes, user flows and site maps to flesh out user experience priorities	
Creation of site look and feel, including 3 rounds of revisions and 1 complete change of direction (if needed)	
Project Management and client communication	
Configuration of Drupal website, including:	$XXX
Installation and configuration of Drupal CMS;	
Establishment of user roles and permissions, including content editors and administrators;	
Project Management and client communication	
Theming of Drupal website, including:	$XXX
Application of site look and feel across all site page templates.	
Creation of up to 5 unique page templates, e.g., Custom homepage templates or interior section templates.	
Estimate Total: $XXXXX	

Section 5.0: the zen kitchen Background & Capabilities

Section 5.1 Who is the zen kitchen?

the zen kitchen combines creative problem-solving with solid business sense and a passion for sustainability to create beautiful, elegant and powerful marketing communi- cations for our clients. the zen kitchen is a small strategic design studio with big project experience that combines a passion for sustainable design and a holistic approach to creativity with clients who make a difference. We work with you closely to uncover the truth behind your unique story and communicate it clearly, elegantly, and effectively to the people you need to hear it.

Section 5.2 What can the zen kitchen do for you?

the zen kitchen has strong experience in creative project management and maintains a strong, nimble network of writers, photographers, programmers, illustrators, printers, and fabricators... to help you scale up to any size project without the costly overhead of larger agencies. From concept to execution, we can give you everything you need—and nothing you don't. Our capabilities include:

- Identity and brand standards systems design;
- Website design, including Wordpress and Drupal development;
- Print collateral design including: annual reports, restaurant menus, brochures, corporate communications, sustainability reports, and capital campaigns;
- Packaging design for food and personal care;
- Environmental graphics and display design.

Section 5.3 Why choose the zen kitchen?

We like to think our approach to marketing and design is simple: just ask questions. But beyond that, we think it's important to ask the right questions, and listen carefully for the answers. Anyone can figure out who your target audience is. Figuring out what's relevant to them, and shaping your messaging to fit that relevance without coming across as inauthentic or cheesy—or worse, being accused of greenwashing? That's what we do best. When you work with the zen kitchen, you get:

Intuitive chefs who help you make the most of what you've got. An intuitive chef never obsesses over a recipe. She knows the ingredients so well she can taste the combinations in her mouth, creating something spectacular with whatever's on hand. We do that for your brand. First, we help you understand what your audience really wants, and then we use fonts, logos, colors, and content to create an experience that matches what you give your customers.

Friendly straight-shooters who get things done—and done right. It's impossible for us to settle for anything less than delightful. And we won't let our clients settle, either. Hid- den beneath this friendly, approachable exterior is a relent- less commitment to your customers. Yes, we're pushy. But don't worry—we know you'll thank us later.

6.0 Terms and Conditions

This work agreement is based on the specifications listed in the above Project Scope. If, upon receipt of all materials to be supplied by client, the project is determined to differ significantly from the original specifications, the client will be notified promptly and an updated estimate will be produced. This estimate does not include expenses and reimbursements aside from those listed in the Estimated Costs and Project Scope.

If such expenses arise, the client will be informed prior to expenditures made and a separate invoice will be submitted for reimbursement.

Payment Notes

Payment will be made in 5 installments monthly starting upon project signoff. The first installment of *$XXXX* is due before project starts; 4 installments of *$XXXX* each will be due on the fifth of each month starting in March 2011.

All estimates are valid for 30 days from the date of estimate.

Payment Notes:

A finance charge of 5% per month will be applied to overdue balances. A charge of $25 per item will be charged for checks returned by the bank.

Professional Relationship:

In order to provide a rewarding working experience for both Client and Designer, Designer seeks to maintain a professional relationship with the Client. Designer and Client agree to:

- Promptly meet deadlines for producing material, payments, and/or work product and communicate clearly if those deadlines can not be met with alternative timelines for delivery.
- Promptly review and reply to communications from parties involved in this project

Deliverables Timeframe

- Milestones and dates/times will be determined in initial project meeting once contract is approved and deposit is received. Once project starts, a detailed action plan will be submitted to client and we will establish deadlines for delivery on content one piece at a time.
- Failure of client to provide the required materials within the established deadlines will result in a delay of all deliverable deadlines. This delay will be equal to the number of days late the materials were received by the Designer, unless otherwise specified in writing, via e-mail, by Designer.

Additional Terms

Rejection/Cancellation of Project

The client shall not unreasonably withhold acceptance of, or payment for, the project. If, prior to completion of the project, the client observes any nonconformance with the design plan, the Designer must be promptly notified, allowing for necessary corrections. Cancellation or Rejection by Client must be made upon 10 days written notice to Designer. Rejection of the completed project or cancellation during its execution will result in forfeiture of the deposit and billing for all additional labor or expenses incurred prior to the date of cancellation, at the standard rate of $*XXX* per hour.

All elements created by the Designer for the project must then be returned to the Designer within 30 days of cancellation. All materials supplied by the Client will be returned in their original condition within 30 days of cancellation. Any usage by the Client of design elements created by the Designer after cancellation of the project will result in appropriate legal action. Client shall bear all costs, expenses, and reasonable attorney's fees in any action brought to recover payment, enforce the terms and or protect Designer's Intellectual Property under this contract.

Designer reserves the right to cancel this contract at any time upon 10 days written notice for any reason, including but not limited to: clients failure to provide materials or payment within 30 days of the agreed upon deadlines or failure of client to comply with the terms of this agreement including the terms of the Professional Relationship clause. Upon Designer's cancellation of the contract, Designer will return all unused funds and deposits to the Client and return all materials to the Client within 30 days of cancellation.

Modifications

Modification of the Agreement must be written, except that the invoice may include, and the Client shall pay, any fees or expenses that were orally authorized by the Client in order to progress promptly with the work. Oral agreements and other communications will be confirmed in writing, including electronically, and thereby incorporated into this agreement.

Ownership of Artwork

The Designer retains ownership of all original artwork, whether preliminary or final. No use of same shall be made, nor any ideas obtained therefrom used, except upon compensation to be determined by the Designer. The client shall return such artwork within thirty (30) days of use. In the case of logo work, the client shall retain ownership of artwork once the invoice has been paid in full and can use said logo in all of their materials, including materials created by other designers. Said artwork, however, may not be modified for any use without the express consent of the Designer.

The Designer retains the right to use the completed project and any preliminary designs for the purpose of design competitions, future publications on design, educational purposes, and marketing materials. Where applicable the client will be given any necessary credit for usage of the project elements.

Reproduction of Work

The client assumes full reproduction rights upon payment for completed project. The work may be reproduced as is by the client at any given time. Any revisions to the work prior to reproduction must be negotiated between the Designer and the client.

Author's Alterations (AA's)

AA's represent work performed in addition to the original concept and specifications. Such work includes, but is not limited to: inclusion of material in project in addition to material originally discussed; additional design concepts or revisions of project beyond the number allotted in the project scope section of this contract; significant color/paper/quantity changes beyond what was originally discussed.

Such additional work shall be charged at a rate of $*XXX* per hour plus any additional expenses incurred by the extra work (including rush shipping and/or printing charges), and will be supported with documentation upon request.

No additional payment shall be made for minor changes required to conform to the original assignment description as noted in the creative brief, including spelling and grammatical errors.

The terms of this paragraph do not apply to the agreed upon alterations, modifications, or edits listed in the Deliverables TimeFrame.

The Designer shall not be held responsible for delays in production caused by Author's Alterations.

Proofs

Proofs will be sent to Client via e-mailed PDF unless otherwise noted in the Project Scope section of this contract. Client will be responsible for carefully reviewing said proofs and offering feedback in a timely and constructive manner. Delays in receipt of appropriate feedback by Client will result in delay of project deliverables. A reasonable variation in color between color proofs and the completed job shall constitute acceptable delivery. The Designer cannot be held responsible for errors under any or all of the following conditions: if the Client has failed to return proofs with indication of changes; if the Client has failed to approve proofs in writing via e-mail or signed Approval Form; if the Client has instructed the Designer to proceed without submission of proofs.

Completion/Delivery of Project

The estimated completion date of the project is to be determined. Any shipping or insurance costs will be assumed by the client. Any alteration or deviation from the above specifications involving extra costs will be executed only upon approval with the client. Any delay in the completion of the project due to failure of client to meet the deadlines set forth in this contract for receipt of materials to begin work on the project, proof revisions/approvals, etc. will delay the completion/delivery date. The Client will allow a reasonable time for printing and shipping of final project (generally 2-3 weeks). The Client will be responsible for any "rush charges" assessed by the printer and/or shipping company due to failure of client to meet the deadlines set forth in this contract for receipt of materials, proof revisions/approvals, etc.

In addition, unusual transportation delays, unforeseen illness, or external forces beyond the control of the Designer, shall entitle the Designer to extend the completion/delivery date, upon notifying the client, by the time equivalent to the period of such delay.

Releases

The Client shall indemnify the Designer against all claims and expenses, including reasonable attorneys' fees, due to uses of design or art work, for which no release was requested in writing or for uses that exceed authority granted by a release. The Client further indemnifies the Designer against any liability, clients, or rights of any third party arising out of this contract, including reasonable attorney's fees and expenses. Client is liable for any costs, including attorney's fees, incurred by Designer in enforcing this agreement and any of its terms.

Any revisions to the work prior to reproduction must be negotiated between the Designer and the client.

Limitation of Liability

The Client agrees that it shall not hold the Designer or his/her agents or employees liable for any incidental or consequential damages which may arise from the Designer's failure to perform any aspect of the Project in a timely manner, regardless of whether such failure was caused by intentional or negligent acts or omissions of the Designer or a third party.

Warranty of Originality

The Designer warrants and represents that, to the best of his/her knowledge, the work assigned hereunder is original and has not been previously published, that consent to use has been obtained on an unlimited basis; the undersigned from third parties is original or, if previously published, that consent to use has been obtained on an unlimited basis; that the Designer has full authority to make this agreement; and that the work prepared by the Designer does not contain any scandalous, libelous, or unlawful matter.

This warranty does not extend to any uses that the Client or others may make of the Designer's product that may infringe on the rights of others. Client expressly agrees that it will hold the Designer harmless for all liability caused by the Client's use of the Designer's product to the extent that such use may infringe on the rights of others.

About the Author

Dani Nordin is an independent user experience designer and strategist who specializes in smart, human-friendly design for progressive brands. She discovered design purely by accident as a Theatre student at Rhode Island College in 1995, and has been doing some combination of design, public speaking and writing ever since.

Dani is a regular feature at Boston's Drupal meetup, and is a regular speaker at Boston's Design for Drupal Camp. In 2011, she was one of several contributors to *The Definitive Guide to Drupal 7* (Apress); the *Drupal for Designers* series is her second book project. You can check out some of her work at tzk-design.com (*http://tzk-design.com*). She also blogs almost regularly at daninordin.com (*http://daninordin.com*).

Dani lives in Watertown, MA with her husband Nick, and Persephone, a 14-pound ~~giant ball of black furry love~~ cat. Both are infinite sources of comedic gold.

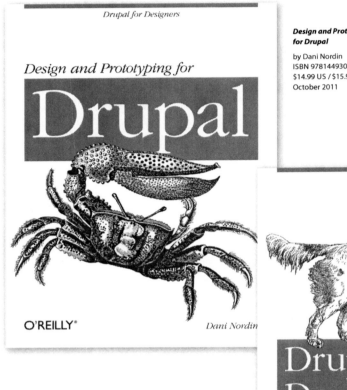

The information you need, when and where you need it.

With Safari Books Online, you can:

Access the contents of thousands of technology and business books

- Quickly search over 7000 books and certification guides
- Download whole books or chapters in PDF format, at no extra cost, to print or read on the go
- Copy and paste code
- Save up to 35% on O'Reilly print books
- **New!** Access mobile-friendly books directly from cell phones and mobile devices

Stay up-to-date on emerging topics before the books are published

- Get on-demand access to evolving manuscripts.
- Interact directly with authors of upcoming books

Explore thousands of hours of video on technology and design topics

- Learn from expert video tutorials
- Watch and replay recorded conference sessions

Get even more for your money.

Join the O'Reilly Community, and register the O'Reilly books you own. It's free, and you'll get:

- $4.99 ebook upgrade offer
- 40% upgrade offer on O'Reilly print books
- Membership discounts on books and events
- Free lifetime updates to ebooks and videos
- Multiple ebook formats, DRM FREE
- Participation in the O'Reilly community
- Newsletters
- Account management
- 100% Satisfaction Guarantee

Signing up is easy:

1. Go to: oreilly.com/go/register
2. Create an O'Reilly login.
3. Provide your address.
4. Register your books.

Note: English-language books only

To order books online:
oreilly.com/store

For questions about products or an order:
orders@oreilly.com

To sign up to get topic-specific email announcements and/or news about upcoming books, conferences, special offers, and new technologies:
elists@oreilly.com

For technical questions about book content:
booktech@oreilly.com

To submit new book proposals to our editors:
proposals@oreilly.com

O'Reilly books are available in multiple DRM-free ebook formats. For more information:
oreilly.com/ebooks

Spreading the knowledge of innovators   oreilly.com

CPSIA information can be obtained at www.ICGtesting.com
Printed in the USA
BVOW042233121011

273481BV00013B/40/P